I give birth to the universe

Tessa Smits

I give birth to the universe

Novel based on a true story

COLOPHON
Are you curious to learn more or want to connect with like-minded individuals?
Follow Tessa on Facebook at https://www.facebook.com/tessasmits.artist or visit her website at www.tessasmits.com.

Copyright © 2023 Tessa Smits
Author: Tessa Smits
First Printing Translation: August 2024
Cover Design: Ruben Lourens & Drawing by Tessa Smits
Illustrations: Tessa Smits
Interior Design: Ruben Lourens
Editing & translation: Eleanor McKenzie
Poem Chapter 37 Translated by: Melanta Ayon & Camie Bonger
Printing: Amazon KDP

Autobiographical Novel
ISBN: 978-90-833667-6-0
NUR: 341

No part of this publication may be reproduced, including but not limited to printing, photocopying, and storage in computerized databases, without prior written permission from the author.

Disclosure:
The insights shared in this book are based on the author's personal experiences and are intended for enrichment and inspiration, not as a substitute for professional medical or psychological advice. Readers are encouraged to think independently and, where necessary, seek professional help. The publisher and author are not liable for any direct or indirect consequences of applying the information contained in this book. This is an autobiographical novel; 95% of it is based on true events. For the remaining 5%, I have taken poetic license to describe things slightly differently, combine characters, or omit certain details. No rights can be derived from this story.

I give birth to the universe

This book is dedicated to the "crazy ones"–the dreamers, the lovers, and the visionaries. It's for anyone who has ever felt out of place, as if they were born on the wrong planet. For those who see the world through a different lens and wonder if they're alone in their experiences. You are not!

Another reality exists. It is unfamiliar to you now, but its potential lies within you and when you discover it, you will be astonished. As you turn these pages, I hope you feel your dormant desires reawaken, that a relentless fire ignites within you, and a profound connection to the universe emerges. Let's cast aside conformity and rules. Forget structure and embrace the sublime chaos that frees the mind.

It's time to unlock your potential: within yourself and in the world!

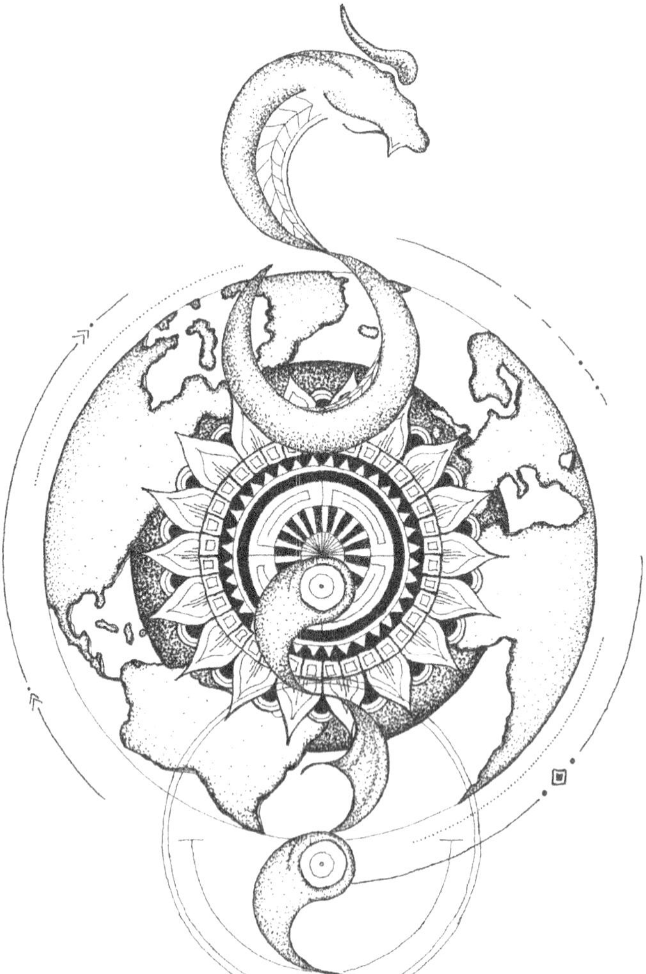

Chapter 1
Nothing Left To Lose

Can you feel it, too? The immense potential we possess as humanity? The extraordinary things we can achieve when we are utterly free from all the shackles we've bound ourselves with? Free from fear, limiting beliefs and thoughts, rules, laws, and frameworks.

When I tap into this vision and feeling, the possibilities are endless. It is an unknown space that is undeniably real. Don't ask me where this came from within me, but I have always felt it, seen it, known it. Even as a child, I fantasised about it and knew with crystal clarity that the world I was living in was not the same as the world that I sensed.

But I didn't yet know a way to get there.

So, I followed the same path as everyone else. I pursued education, eventually ending up at the prestigious Nyenrode university. I started carving out a career within the confines of an office.

Despite the promise of a comfortable future, I felt a dissonance each day, a persistent sense that something far better awaited beyond the familiar. I sensed that life could be radically different. However, the vastness of the unknown was intimidating, so I attempted to suppress it, to bury it deep within. But neglecting one's inner truth gradually extinguishes the soul's flame. Day by day, little by little, you dim your inner light.

Burnout or bore out–it doesn't matter what we label it. I

believe that today's widespread fatigue and severe mental health issues share a root cause. Deep down, we all sense that we're not meant to be living this way. Spending our days in fluorescent-lit offices from 9 to 5, engaging in work that lacks soul, only to return home exhausted, collapse in front of a Netflix series, mindlessly devour something for dinner, and then drag ourselves to bed. And we repeat this cycle day in, day out, for months, year after year. It simply makes no sense! It's destructive. We're becoming sicker, heavier, more exhausted, apathetic, irritable, and more disconnected from ourselves than ever before.

After experiencing my own wake-up call–a burnout at around age 30–I started a business. The idea was to create a space where I could set my own rules and maintain my freedom. I had a crystal-clear vision of what I needed to do: I wanted to establish a sanctuary where people could reconnect with their souls, find peace, and rediscover their own energy. A place dedicated to true collaboration and creativity.

I laid the concept out on paper within a day: a complete business plan requiring an investment of two million dollars. Almost immediately, I dismissed it as delusions of grandeur and cast the plan aside. It seemed too impossible. It made more sense to start with what I knew. I would capitalise on my marketing skills to earn money. Once I had made my first million on my own, I would have the freedom and the means to pursue what I truly felt I was meant to do in this world.

Things turned out differently. I found freedom, but not in the carefree, wealthy existence that I had imagined. My so-called genius marketing idea was an online platform for conferences and seminars. Unfortunately, just after its launch, the financial market collapsed, plunging us into years of financial crisis. The market for congresses and seminars was among the first to grind to a halt. In fact, only a month after launching, I found myself bankrupt on paper. However, giving up was not an option for me, so I doubled my efforts to clear all the debts. For years, I went without vacations and lived without excess spending, barely making ends meet every month. Freedom seemed more elusive than ever; I felt trapped, unable to move forward.

After seven years, just as I was nearing the end of paying off my debt, disaster struck. My client declared bankruptcy, leaving my invoices unpaid. With no reserves to fall back on, I too went bankrupt and lost everything. Yet, it was there, in that moment of losing it all, that I truly discovered freedom for the first time. Nothing left to lose truly meant having absolutely nothing left to lose. Suddenly, I felt liberated to do anything, pursue anything, because I couldn't fall any further. I was already at rock bottom, having experienced a profound failure.

I had become Ultimately Free.

During this period, fueled by that renewed sense of freedom and despite being at my lowest, I wrote my first book: *'Bankruptcy, It Doesn't Get Any Sweeter.'*

The publication of this book marked the beginning of a new adventure. I was clear about my destination: a world where I could create anything, a realm where I could achieve the infinite. I knew it was possible because I had seen it, felt it, and known it for so long. The reality was that after seven years of repaying debts, I had become completely drained. I still had just enough energy to get out of bed, and that was about it. In retrospect, this was a blessing. Had I possessed the strength to rebuild my safe, limited life around marketing work, I suspect that the craving for security might have ultimately triumphed over the yearning for a real, albeit unknown, life.

No, I simply couldn't go on; a blessing in disguise, you could say. I found myself literally homeless, with nothing but a few suitcases and an old car to my name. After spending months on the couches and in the attics of friends, it was my sister and my brother-in-law who provided me with a lifeline. They invited me to live with them in Spain, in their spacious finca. They asked for nothing in return, giving me the opportunity to truly relax, recuperate, and rediscover myself.

I seized the opportunity with both hands. Now, I was truly leaving everything behind: everything familiar, everything that had provided even the slightest sense of security. I moved to a country whose language I did not speak, where the only person I knew was my sister. Now, I was living on a mountain, in the middle of nowhere....

Chapter 2
I Don't Need To Do Anything

Many people dream and fantasise about it: sitting atop a mountain, reflecting on your life, arriving at profound self-insights, and then descending the mountain enlightened. I spent years on that mountain attempting to find myself, yet anger consumed me towards a world that I felt had betrayed me. Despite working tirelessly and pouring my entire self into my efforts, my hard work was not rewarded but punished.

I felt forsaken by a world that preached the gospel of hard work as the key to the future.

So, I found myself particularly grumpy on that mountain, extending a defiant middle finger to the world below as I decided to opt out. Of course, I also felt angry for allowing myself to be swept up in a system I never truly believed in. I had repeatedly pushed beyond my limits, working tirelessly to stave off bankruptcy. I ignored physical ailments and accepted yet another assignment. And for what? In the end, I lost everything: my house in Amsterdam, my relationship, my job, my very identity. But most of all, I had let myself down. For years, I ignored my intuition, engaging in work that made me unhappy, and making everything about money and survival. I hadn't truly lived for years, throwing away precious time for nothing. Yet, facing this realisation was even more painful. Initially, that's why I primarily directed my anger at the outside world.

'I'm out of the game!'
'Figure it out with that stupid system!'
And with that, I angrily stayed where I was seated.

But here's the funny thing: no matter how intense your anger might be, the world simply continues on without you. And after all my ranting and raving, which only succeeded in temporarily scattering some butterflies and birds, I knew I had to come to terms with myself.

When I had just arrived in Spain, I would wake up every morning already overwhelmed by a barrage of thoughts about what I should do next to prevent complete chaos. My mind craved control, but I was completely exhausted. So, the only thing I told myself every morning was, 'I don't have to do anything'.

I repeated that mantra until I truly felt it, granting myself sincere permission: 'I don't need to do anything, even if the whole world collapses. I need nothing more than to feel what truly arises from within me and to follow that feeling, whatever it may be! Even if it means sitting on the couch every day, watching movies, or simply staring into space. It's all good.'

This will make your head spin, I assure you. It brought up panicked thinking: 'If I surrender to this, I will accomplish nothing and eventually perish!'

But I didn't perish. Instead, I asked myself earnestly: 'What do I feel like doing? What will naturally unfold on its own?'

For the first few weeks, the answer was that very little happened; I was, metaphorically, at my end. So, I spent my days lying on the couch, watching movies. Was I truly allowed to liberate myself to this extent? Could I grant myself the space to explore what was present without judgment, hurry, or a predefined plan? And with no idea where this journey was leading?

It didn't come naturally. I frequently reverted to thinking

and analysing. But no matter how desperately my mind clamoured for safety and security; no matter how much I yearned to regain control and how often I secretly considered conforming to the system once more, it was no longer an option.

The lid was already off the pot. The spark had ignited, and the fire was intensifying. I was determined to be myself, regardless of the consequences! That realisation sent a surge of bliss through me that was without parallel. The mere thought of being true to myself was exhilarating.

F*ck society!
If it means I don't fit in, so be it.
If it means I won't earn the big money, I will accept that.

I want to feel alive, embrace who I am, and fully love the incredible woman I feel is within myself.

Chapter 3
What If I Can Do Anything?

I had said yes to myself and to a new way of living, but I had no idea what that new way was going to look like. How could I ensure I wouldn't just revert to my old ways? I mean, returning to the routine of earning money in an office for forty hours a week. That life, that kind of existence, was something I didn't want to return to. But when that's all you know, and you believe it's the only way to make a living, it's all too easy to find yourself in a slightly different job, yet walking the same path once again...

How can I conceive of something unknown to me?

With that question in mind, I climbed the mountain every day, driven by curiosity. Having lost everything, I had nothing left to lose. It was a stroke of genius: many people hesitate to try something new because of various responsibilities–be it children, a mortgage, a sick mother, or an outstanding bill. They're held back from exploring the unfamiliar, with outcomes that are unpredictable. However, my bankruptcy put me in a uniquely advantageous position. I had already faced failure, which meant I could no longer fail. Having nothing in my account meant I had nothing to lose either. And now, here I was in a foreign country, not speaking the language, sitting on a mountain without even a dog for company. In this setting, devoid of any external stimuli, I pondered: What would spontaneously arise from within me? What would my true role be if I stopped allowing myself to be shaped by the external world? If I could momentarily disregard all rules, laws, and political correctness, and wipe my mind of everything I've learned, what would happen? Would the real Tessa then come to light?

Well, I can tell you, the real Tessa remained quite silent for a while. It was as if she was thinking: 'Let's see if she truly means it.' Revealing your true self is a daunting endeavor. What if I allowed myself to emerge and then lacked the courage to embrace it? That would be a profound betrayal of myself. So, weeks turned into months amidst the olive trees.

Completely engulfed in boredom, truly feeling the dullness seep into my cells, I rose about six months later with a sudden decision to paint. Don't ask me where the impulse came from. I simply felt inspired by an image that had lingered in my mind for years, wondering if I could transfer it onto a canvas. It was a thought that had never occurred to me before, which intrigued me instantly. Painting? Me? I had never engaged in anything creative before.

At the local paint store, I picked up some basic colours and a canvas. With my newly purchased brush in hand, I began applying the first colours to the canvas, stroke by stroke. The geometric shape that had lingered in my mind for years suddenly sprang to life. My enthusiasm grew with each brushstroke. As the colours blended on the canvas, I gradually found myself again. I felt a surge of pleasure that had been absent for far too long. Astonishment flowed through me, a kind of reacquaintance with a part of myself that had never before made itself known. And when the painting was complete, I felt a sense of pride that I hadn't experienced in years.

I had created something entirely on my own! Something that had not existed before, something that nobody had requested of me, and yet, I had brought it to life on canvas. What an extraordinary sensation.

This experience propelled me to explore further. With no background in painting or art creation, I turned to YouTube for some online education. I immersed myself in video after video, watching artists craft the most beautiful works with hundreds of different techniques. I became instantly obsessed. The freedom of creation, the colours, the movements, the intensity–it was all so captivating! I yearned to experience this freedom and creativity for myself.

Without overthinking, I started experimenting with various media, patterns, and drawing techniques. I also ventured into working with drops of paint. Creating something one paint drop at a time ushered me into a meditative state. Hours passed with ease, my mind quieted, and I immersed myself in pure feeling, being, silence, and wonder. I didn't think, I simply allowed myself to be swept up in the flow of creation.

Chapter 4
Creating In Full Surrender

Painting ignited something within me. I felt a surge of fresh energy, but more importantly, I uncovered something invaluable that marked the start of a journey beyond my wildest dreams. I realised then that by fully surrendering to my intuition during painting, giving no thought to what I was going to create, I could produce works of art that my mind alone could never have conceived in a lifetime.

Embracing painting with complete surrender wasn't a simple task. It demanded that I remain open and relinquish control. Could anything and everything emerge? Was I permitted to create something deemed ugly? Was failure an option? As I navigated these weeks of experimentation, striving to stay in the flow without premeditating the outcome, I occasionally shared my journey on Facebook. And - as if by design, though coincidence seems to play no part - this led me to connect with a Dutch artist living just a few mountains away, Elske.

After a few phone calls, she spontaneously suggested we meet for a cup of coffee. Intrigued by this turn of events, I immediately agreed, and that very afternoon, she drove up the mountain in her old Renault.

Imagine a small, petite woman, dressed in an Indonesian-style outfit, and you've pictured Elske. Upon seeing her, I instantly knew we were going to be friends! It felt as though we had known each other for years. After the initial 'how did you end up here in Spain?' conversation, we quickly delved into discussions about art creation.

Elske's father was an artist. This gave her the opportunity to develop her painting technique from an early age. Her explanation of her approach to art mesmerised me. She, too, painted purely intuitively, without planning a design in advance, tuning into a subject and simply allowing her brush to glide across the canvas. She took out her phone to show me some of her paintings. They were stunning: featuring beautiful soft shapes, immeasurable depth, and an intense use of colour.

When I inquired about how she created these magical canvases, she explained her process to me. She described seeing herself as an instrument through which inspiration flowed naturally. It simply happened.

I completely understood where she was coming from. After all, I had experienced the same magic in the weeks prior–the magic that unfolds when everything is allowed to exist and flow freely. Sometimes it appeared the ideas and images originated from another realm. A world invisible to the eye, yet tangibly present. Sometimes, I even felt as if I were connecting with the future.

It was challenging not to overthink this phenomenon, so encountering someone who had the same experience was incredibly reassuring. Elske and I understood each other immediately, with no need to explain our feelings or thoughts. The most beautiful creations emerged when we minimised our own presence, to the point where we no longer mattered, and served solely as conduits.

As we spent hours sharing our experiences with this intuitive way of working, an idea took shape. It was an idea that would mark the start of the rollercoaster journey I had unknowingly embarked upon. Together, we decided to undertake an experiment–an experiment in which we would let go of everything, clear our minds, and begin creating as one. We were going to play!

Chapter 5
The Experiment

We didn't hesitate. Just a few days later, we found ourselves on the terrace, basking in a typically warm southern Spanish winter day. By nine o'clock, the morning sun was already warming our skin, the wind tousled our hair, and the scent of burnt wood lingered in the air... our faces had a look of slight tension.

There we stood, side by side, in front of a large table draped with a white cloth measuring one metre by one metre. Tubes of paint, showcasing every colour of the rainbow, awaited us. The freshly washed brushes sparkled in the morning sunlight, and the pots of water beside them were crystal clear.

We had agreed in advance not to set any specific expectations. Instead, we committed to the intention of creating something entirely new together. We accepted everything could go right or wrong (though 'wrong' no longer existed in our approach), and we were open to every possibility. In a state of complete surrender to and with each other, we aimed to create something unique. To reinforce this mindset, we selected a meditation to begin our morning. Through this, we hoped to connect more easily with each other and with the vision of what we were about to create. We also intended that the meditation would help us quiet our minds a bit.

Well, quieting the mind.

After the meditation, we sat in silence, staring ahead.

What had seemed like a brilliant idea now felt unsettlingly uncomfortable.

'Can I truly let go with someone else present?' I wondered, glancing at Elske.

'What if we end up creating something truly ugly and waste all that paint?' Elske muttered, more to herself than to me.

Gradually, I reached for a brush on the table and felt myself being drawn toward the color red.

'Opening up to everything' I realized that not knowing made me nervous. Yet, alongside this nervousness, I felt an immense curiosity and joy.

'What exists beyond my current comprehension?' I pondered.

'I trust in everything,' I assured myself. 'I surrender to the process. Nothing beautiful is required to emerge; everything is permitted, nothing is obligatory.'

As I plunged my brush deeply into the pot of red paint, I repeated aloud a few times, "Everything is allowed; nothing is mandatory."

Feeling convinced, I drew the first line on the canvas. I didn't restrain the stroke; instead, I let it wander freely across the canvas, feeling a surge of great pleasure bubbling up within me. 'This is fun!' I thought, smiling as I dipped my brush into the paint for a second time. Now, it felt even easier to just let go and create. Red-a colour of passion, heat, excitement, and thrills-how wonderful!

Then, out of nowhere, Elske boldly dragged her blue across my red streak.

'What!!!' my mind screamed. 'What are you doing?'

But I quickly reminded myself: 'Oh yes, wait, everything is allowed, nothing is wrong. Is everything truly allowed to emerge?'

    Letting go, I watched as her blue and my red mixed, creating an intense purple where they met. 'Ah, yes, what a beautiful colour!' I thought, feeling an immediate desire to expand the purple across the canvas. Together, we blended our colours into a beautiful purple sphere. Then I swiftly added some yellow to create a contrasting area next to the new stripes. Ideas and inspiration surged within me like a swirling river. Without consciously thinking, I sensed what could be painted. I wasn't directing anything; instead, I was surrendering to the colours and shapes.

Elske and I didn't speak a word; we became one with the canvas, the paint, and whatever was unfolding. Colour combinations I normally wouldn't choose came to life. It felt right; it was vibrant.

Painting together resembled a dance,
moving around each other,
intuitively knowing when to pause and when to proceed,
occasionally stepping back to let the canvas guide us toward the next move.

The painting evolved into a world of its own. Different layers and dimensions emerged effortlessly, blurring the lines between fantasy and reality. Yet, everything felt harmoniously right, as if it were a home, unified with everything.
    Hours slipped by, the sun dipped behind the mountains, and as our warmed bodies cooled, it marked ten hours of creation. When we added the final details, it felt like waking from a dream.

Slowly, we placed our brushes into the murky water and both stepped back. The canvas dried quickly in the warm Spanish evening, and soon we could prop it upright against the wall.

Exhausted, we collapsed to the ground together. I pulled my legs up and gently lowered my chin to my knees, utterly enchanted by the creation before us.

Two worlds seemed to merge; I saw a dragon, fire, and a globe adorned with ancient symbols (had I placed them there?). The colour transitions captivated my gaze, refusing to release it. The painting unfolded a story.

Glancing at Elske, I noticed tears in her eyes, moved by the artwork just as I was.

"I could never have imagined this on my own," she whispered.

"No, neither could I," I responded, my own eyes firmly fixed on the canvas, equally spellbound.

"This is magic! An actual creation. It feels so real," she exclaimed in surprise.

"I know!" I was just as euphoric about what had unfolded in the past few hours.

"Els, this is how we, as humans, can create the most amazing things!" I said, brimming with enthusiasm.

"Just imagine if we always created together in such connection, with such surrender, drawing from each of our unique talents and gifts. What genius things would we then be capable of?"

"Yes, infinite possibilities," Elske replied, her gaze still fixed on the painting

Despite being on a deserted, olive-covered mountain, I stood up and exclaimed as if I were addressing a global audience, "This is creation! If only we dare to let go, and not remain in our limited thinking!"

"Yes, but we are, Tess," Elske remarked dryly.

Unperturbed, I continued, "But we don't have to! Look at what we can do in one day, with pure intention. Then, surely, this should also be possible in our daily lives! Work, relationships, and living–it could all be so connected. Surely, it must be possible to create a life that does not exist now, but which we have long known is possible?"

"I don't know if it's that easy," said Elske soberly, "but I do know that this is a great painting. Come, let's take some pictures."

"You know what I'd love?" I said as Elske set the canvas down for a nice composition. "If only more people could see it, instead of it just hanging in someone's living room. This energy, this power of our synergy, is for everyone!"

"Synergy? How about naming it Synergia?" Elske suggested, as she took detailed pictures of the canvas. Then she stopped for a moment, as if my words were only now reaching her. "Yes, I agree with you. This canvas has something to tell, and it would be nice to hang it somewhere where more people come, like a yoga studio or something."

"Yes, let's give the canvas that intention."

As Elske made a Facebook post, I was still gripped by the idea that this could very well be just the tip of the iceberg. Of course, Elske was right; this was not easy. A safe, creative experiment on a mountain was really quite different from applying this to your daily life. But I couldn't let go of the idea; I had to explore it. What if this could really happen? What if I dared to live and create with this inspiration? Then what might I be capable of? I could feel the potentiality without knowing exactly what it meant. I had to explore this!

"Tess, you won't believe it!" Elske rudely pulled me back to reality as she enthusiastically waved her phone in front of my face.

Her hopping made it impossible for me to read anything on the screen as it moved back and forth in front of my eyes. "What?" I asked impatiently.

"The painting has been sold!" she exclaimed, enthusiastically waving her phone in front of my face. "I posted it less than five minutes ago, and already there is someone who wants to buy it!"

"No way!" I grabbed the phone out of her hands and scrolled through the comments. The painting received a massive number of likes, and yes, there it was. Someone wanted the painting, and I knew who it was.

"That's Ronald, from Seats2Meet! So, the painting will hang in his co-working location. My goodness, Els, do you know what this means?" Before she could say anything back, I rattled on. "This canvas is going to be seen by thousands of people a year. In a place all about synergy. I mean, Ronald is the visionary of new ways of working together, connecting with each other." By now, I wasn't even talking in full sentences anymore.

"Oh my god!" Elske exclaimed. What I was saying was now sinking in. "Within five minutes, we've manifested the thing we set our intention on."

"Yes, exactly!" I looked at her smugly. "So, this is possible if you dare to create in surrender. This is what I mean, Els; this is just the beginning!"

"Now, now." Elske had to laugh at all my enthusiasm, as she wasn't so convinced yet.

But I was.
This was it; this is what I was going to do!

Chapter 6
Behind The Veils Of Illusion

In the days that followed, this idea haunted me. What could I do to make this a reality? How could I relinquish my thoughts and truly surrender? Could I–without over analysing–create a life where I live up to my full potential? I had often read about the importance of 'trust' and 'going with the flow of life,' but how could I achieve this?

My curiosity about unlimited possibilities led me to explore the work of several neuroscience experts. Their research reveals how we often limit ourselves through endlessly recurring patterns, preventing us from utilising our full capabilities. It also illuminates how we can reprogram ourselves to tap into our 'infinite' powers.

In essence, every experience you've had in your life is encoded within the cells of your body. Thus, when you encounter a similar situation anew, your body's response mirrors that of the first experience. Consider how a piece of music from the past can instantly transport you back to the emotions associated with your first love. It is through these stored patterns that you shape the world around you, determine your reactions, and take your actions. Consequently, you often repeat the same behaviours, effectively running around in circles within your life. If you're someone who has historically had limited financial resources, you might find yourself stuck in that pattern. Similarly, if maintaining long-term relationships has always been a challenge, this pattern may persist. This happens because your system–comprising your beliefs and experiences–

accepts these circumstances as unchangeable truths. Consequently, you unconsciously expect that things will always remain the same, especially if you lack other examples to learn from.

Reflecting on my life, I recognized how childhood experiences instilled persistent patterns in me, such as believing 'you have to work hard for your money,' 'life isn't always fun,' or 'you can't trust anyone.' These examples are just the tip of the iceberg. Fortunately, scientists have proposed an intriguing solution: it's possible to reprogram the information stored in your cells. The key lies in convincing your body that a different reality is possible.

This idea captivated me deeply; I felt in my core that it was the answer I had been searching for. It presented an opportunity to think outside the traditional boundaries, going a step beyond concepts like 'the law of attraction'. The studies illustrate that to truly undergo a fresh experience, one must wholeheartedly believe in its possibility. This is challenging, however, because deeply ingrained beliefs, such as the conviction that one will never have a loving relationship, live in the unconscious part of our brain. It is not possible to switch off these beliefs by merely adopting a temporarily positive mindset. Mere wishing does not equate to the genuine belief that your reality can be different. This is the critical issue.

Yet, the question remains: How can one genuinely believe in the possibility of a new reality with no reference point or understanding of what it might be like, especially when one has never experienced such a reality? People have crafted many meditations for this very purpose–meditations that guide you into your unconscious to facilitate a new experience that you can immediately internalise.

Upon reading this, I had a realisation: I could immerse myself in books endlessly, but genuine change wouldn't occur unless

I actively engaged with the process. Thus, I downloaded the meditations and dedicated an hour to reprogramming.

One meditation particularly resonated with me; one which stimulated the pineal gland. This gland is the same part of the brain that becomes active with the use of mind-altering substances, such as LSD. Essentially, it quiets the mind, paving the way to more readily embrace new experiences and dimensions.

This seemed like an intriguing meditation to try. I settled on my bed, covered myself with a blanket, and allowed the calm voice of the meditation to guide me. The uplifting music quickly transported me to another realm. As my breathing deepened, I felt myself sinking further and further, still present but merging into everything around me. The energy was tangible. The experience intensified when, halfway through, the voice encouraged me to embrace the unknown, letting go of all preconceived notions.

'Are you in or out?' his deep voice demanded in a commanding tone.

At that moment, I realized I had a decision to make. Could I truly let go and immerse myself in an experience so profoundly different from anything I had known? During the meditation, I knew I was instinctively holding back.

'Reveal the layer of illusion,' the voice in the meditation continued.

Yet, my thought was to take it slow; diving headfirst into the unknown wasn't necessary. My inner sense of caution was still too pronounced to fully give in to the meditation. And that was okay. I've always believed in tuning into your own pace, understanding what feels right. Consequently, I concluded the meditation feeling wonderfully relaxed.

In the weeks that followed, I engaged in this meditation several more times. Each session saw me delving deeper and deeper until a moment of magic unfolded. One Friday night, just before sleep, I decided to immerse myself in the meditation once again. As I reached the midpoint, the familiar question echoed once more, 'Are you in or out?'

This time, a sense of pleasure and curiosity washed over me, prompting me to think: 'Okay, let's do this! Sweep away the veil of illusions! Let's discover what lies beyond.' I was ready to break free from the constraints of my preconceived notions that didn't resonate with my true feelings. 'Bring it on!' I thought.

No sooner had the thought crossed my mind than I felt as though I was plummeting down a roller coaster, accelerating at lightning speed through a realm of multiple dimensions. My physical form seemed to melt away, leaving me with the sensation of non-existence. I soared through galaxies, buoyed by the music and the stirring words of the meditation, and I was still vibrating from the experience for hours afterward while lying in bed. It was as if entirely new knowledge was coursing through me. That night, I slept deeply, transported far beyond my usual dreams.

When I woke up in the morning, I felt good–clear-headed and rested–so I got out of bed in a positive mood to start to the day. After breakfast, I made a quick trip to the supermarket for a few errands. I started my car and drove down the winding road that leads to the village. Upon reaching the village, I headed to Mercadona, a Spanish grocery chain. The parking lot was half-empty when I arrived, so finding a spot was easy. Inside, the robust, salty smell from the extensive fish department was a reminder of our coastal location. Deciding on fresh fish for dinner sounded like a splendid idea, so I ordered three small flounders, my favourite. With my basket now half full, I made my way to the checkout line.

And then it happened!

One moment I was standing in line, staring blankly ahead, and the next, a sensation of unity with everything around me overwhelmed me. In that moment, I was there, fully immersed in this profound experience. I felt connected to the cash register, the people, the baskets–everything, because… I WAS EVERYTHING!!

I embodied the cash register, myself, the people nearby, and even the shelves stocked with products. At that instant, I merged with the world around me.

I burst out laughing loudly. So this was it! My laughter grew as I realised how utterly impractical it was to have this experience in the real world. Just as quickly as I had entered this state of oneness, I snapped back out of it.

A Spanish man in front of me turned around, giving me a questioning look.

"Nada," I muttered, continuing to giggle.

I know, it sounds too bizarre! But you don't have to take my word for it; anyone who has experienced this for themselves will understand. They just know it's the truth. However, this experience isn't an end goal, but it reveals that if everything is truly one, then nothing is separate. That means the individual self, as an entity, doesn't exist in that state of oneness. Yet, here on Earth, we clearly exist as separate individuals, distinct from one another.

Now, I understood that unity existed on another level, and that I could connect with this all-encompassing field and truly feel our interconnectedness. This realisation opened up a realm of unprecedented possibilities. I wondered, what could I achieve by engaging with this energy?

Calling the experience 'mind-blowing' doesn't do it justice. It was such a profound experience that my mind immediately sought to regain control. I analysed the experience, trying to convince myself that it was just a vivid daydream, cautioning against being overly influenced. However, no matter how fervently my mind tried to revert to its former scepticism, it was futile. I had felt it; I had lived it. This was reality!

There was an undeniable joy in this experience because if such a dimension or reality existed, then every concept or belief was not entirely accurate. Everything was simultaneously true and not true. Imagine the level of freedom that comes with this understanding. This transcended the mere sense of liberation one might feel after overcoming a financial crisis. It was about breaking free from every belief entrenched in my mind, from everything I had ever learned in school. This was quantum physics at a most profound level. The sky wasn't the limit anymore; in fact, the concept of 'sky' ceased to exist altogether.

I felt euphoric
as if life itself pulsed through my body
it was an unreal sensation yet it felt more genuine than anything
I had always known this
I smiled from ear to ear
like an adolescent in love, suddenly perceiving the world with fresh wonder
enamoured with life itself, rather than with a lanky, pimply boyfriend.

But, as is often the case with euphoria, a crash followed such a peak experience. The descent was swift and harsh. Fears dominated my nights, and doubts besieged my mind at the thought of letting everything go. 'How will I live? How will I make ends meet? Can I really take care of myself in this way? Why isn't everyone doing this? Am I going crazy?' These were just a few of the questions swirling around in my head.

In the days that followed, I felt both empty and burdened. Netflix became my solace; I gravitated towards movies depicting the complete destruction of the world, which oddly soothed me–a scenario I'm sure an average psychiatrist would find fascinating to analyse.

However, it ultimately didn't matter. I had set the intention; things were in motion, and I realised I truly wasn't in control anymore. The system was adjusting itself.

Breathe in... Breathe out...

Chapter 7
Can I Still Go Back?

Despite facing a harsh backlash, my newfound insight undeniably shifted something within me. As my worst fears receded, my desire for more awareness resurfaced. A few days later, I resumed my morning meditation ritual. Throughout the day, I experimented with my art, eager to capture visually my recent experiences with these dimensions and energies. Gradually, I found myself integrating geometric patterns and unfamiliar symbols into my paintings. They felt significant, though their meaning remained elusive to me.

Starting each day with meditation was rewarding, as it consistently reconnected me with the core feeling from which I wished to live. This feeling of unity with everything, the assurance that everything flows correctly as it should, and a profound curiosity about the unknown. Setting this powerful intention at the start of each day definitely set something in motion.

It was as if opening myself to this desire allowed for a deeper connection, making it increasingly easier to align with this state. For example, one afternoon when I took my car to the garage, I immediately struck up a pleasant conversation with the owner. My command of Spanish was far from perfect, but because I felt so deeply connected, words seemed almost unnecessary. I experienced an intense sense of connection with the people around me. It was as if everyone suddenly started smiling at me, and I could feel joy and relaxation coursing through my body. A realisation struck me: I could indeed navigate life in this manner. It nearly made me leap for joy. My energy had fundamentally shifted as a direct result of my recent practices.

That evening, I settled onto the couch next to my sister and my English brother-in-law, Lee. We tuned into the British news, which, as usual, focused on Brexit. The broadcast was full of stories about the country's struggles, tales of deceit, and the palpable powerlessness felt by the populace. After thirty minutes of absorbing these negative narratives, filled with drama and fear, I was utterly overwhelmed. Couldn't anyone see the harm in routinely exposing ourselves to such energy every night?

Having recently experienced the profound, positive effects of meditation–where my focus was solely on new images and positive experiences–I couldn't help but wonder about the detrimental impact of the opposite. What happens when you consistently absorb negative messages, starting each morning with beliefs like: the world is dangerous, people can't be trusted, everything is a lie? How does that mindset influence the way you approach your day? Would I have engaged in the same open conversation with the mechanic in the garage? Or, influenced by a mindset of mistrust, would I have approached him with scepticism? Could such an attitude even lead to creating a scenario where the mechanic, albeit briefly, confirms that negative belief?

I grew curious about the potential changes in my life if, instead of dedicating half an hour each evening to the news, I nourished myself with other, more enriching information. How would this shift affect my overall wellbeing? Could it possibly alleviate feelings of depression?

To find out, I committed to an experiment. Every time the news was about to air, I chose an activity that enriched me: meditating outside for thirty minutes, taking a stroll, exercising, watching an inspiring documentary or video, dancing, or painting. These activities, I believed, would reconnect me with myself and boost my mood.

In the days that followed, I found that this decision led to unexpected outcomes. I became increasingly sensitive and more in tune with my feelings. While I had previously watched TV almost on autopilot, I now found myself compelled to be more thoughtful about it. This shift also heightened my self-awareness.

    'What am I doing?' I questioned myself as I automatically reached for another bowl of potato chips. Acting decisively, I then poured the rest of the chips into the trash can.

My inner self became more illuminated as I ceased to distract myself with external factors, like the news. With my attention no longer fixated on the world's mistakes, my own actions came into sharp relief.

Shit.
It suddenly dawned on me why this path wasn't for everyone. It demanded taking full responsibility for one's own life, a task only I could undertake for myself.

Could I ever go back?

Chapter 8
Surfing The Wave Of Life

On some days, I experienced the full power of real life, and I rode that wave like a seasoned pro. I felt my connection with everything and everyone around me deeply, moving through life, brimming with inspiration. Those were the days when I created my most beautiful works of art, when ideas flooded in by the hundreds, and I felt love for everyone around me.

But on other days, I was like someone in drug rehab, craving all my old distractions NOW. For me, those were watching TV and indulging in food. I might not have been as drawn to drugs or alcohol, but in the end, it's all the same. Mindless sex, TV, food, and drugs, they're all distractions from truly living, from truly feeling, from being genuinely present. Without my preferred distractions, life felt hard. So, I opened another bag of chips, thinking, 'We'll try feeling again tomorrow.'

It often made me laugh out loud. So, this was what freedom felt like; this was truly living. The flow everyone sought to be part of. This flow actually resembled a wave, and like any wave, it had its ups and downs. I knew this, yet I ignored it. I believed I was in control, convinced I could keep the wave rising indefinitely. That the wave might fall again didn't seem to apply to me! I was determined to always be at the peak, to continue ascending. Let the others be the ones to descend and falter. Not me!

But as I strived to climb higher, I felt resistance mounting within me. I noticed how sluggish I became, how difficult it was to maintain that constant ascent. It required immense willpower to disregard that growing resistance. In that relentless upward pursuit, where I refused to let go, believing I was in control, I looked down upon those who seemed to ride the waves below meekly. I convinced myself that I was different, that my talents were superior, and my intellect was just a notch above the rest. I was determined not to follow the natural ebb and flow, to hold on tight, to hold my breath, to keep holding on, never to let go, for this house of cards must not fall, because if it did, then... oh god, what then?

Failing to move with the flow had utterly exhausted me. I now understood the importance of descending with the wave as well. It was no longer about exerting willpower, but about moving at my body's natural pace. Moving is living. I was facing new rules, ones I hadn't yet grasped. Was everything permissible? Was it okay to have a bad day? To feel uncertain? To not always view the day with optimism? To experience failure? To embrace my humanity? To acknowledge the humanity of others? To relinquish control?

Releasing all those judgments allowed me to fully embrace being myself. The result was an immense sense of relaxation and joy; to call it liberating would be an understatement.

This realisation unleashed a powerful current within me. What would I desire if there were no limits? What dreams had I been harbouring in secret? Joy bubbled up inside me. Gazing at my painting materials, I asked: what did I truly want to achieve with my paint? Suddenly, a thought emerged: I yearned to create something monumental with my art. Not merely a canvas measuring one metre square, but something truly colossal.

I couldn't help but laugh at my rather grandiose aspiration, considering I had only been an artist for a few months. However, I quickly dismissed this thought as a mere limitation. To dream freely truly means embracing boundlessness. There were no constraints; if I wished to create on a grand scale, then why not pursue it?

To bolster this mindset, I embraced another meditation; this one focused on fully realising my potential with no boundaries. The meditation invited me to fully immerse myself in this new reality, asking: 'How does it feel? How are you living? What are you doing?'

   Lost in the meditation, I gave myself over to the exhilaration of conceiving a monumental artwork. My vision was clear, my art fully realised. I envisioned myself using vast quantities of paint, bound by no limits of canvas size. I could feel my body moving as if I were actually creating this massive piece, dancing around it with large pots of paint in my hands, my hair wildly streaming behind me. After the meditation ended, I remained on the couch for a while, basking in the afterglow with a smile on my face. It was a truly wonderful feeling!

Less than a week later, I received a text message from my good friend Sander. He had been on a cycling journey for several weeks and had recently arrived in southern Spain, staying at a retreat centre nearby. In his message, he excitedly told me about the place and mentioned that a great opportunity awaited me. As it turned out, he had spoken about me and my art, and the owner of the retreat centre had inquired if I might be interested in painting the yoga studio floor.

I was utterly astonished. To paint an entire floor! And to think, I had just visualised it! The grand art project I had dreamt of, which I had vividly felt and experienced through my meditations, had now manifested in my reality. With a broad smile, I quickly typed back, expressing my eagerness to take on the project.

The next wave had arrived, and I mounted my board with zeal.

Chapter 9
Paradise

Before I knew it, I had exchanged contact information with Camm, the retreat centre's owner. When I called, an English woman's soft voice greeted me with tales of their special retreat, crafted by hand and in harmony with nature. She explained it was a sanctuary for yoga and that she often collaborated with volunteers to enhance its beauty. We clicked instantly, and she extended an invitation for me to visit. In exchange for my contribution of creating artwork on the yoga floor, she offered me accommodation in one of the wooden cabins and three meals a day.

I didn't have to ponder long before I promised Camm I'd come. Immediately, I packed a bag with some clothes. A suitcase seemed unnecessary, as I anticipated the trip would take only about three days. Unsure of how I would approach this large art project, I brought with me as many work materials as possible: two crates filled with brushes, rulers, sketchbooks, drawing supplies, and the largest compass I owned.

Camm had texted me the location, and it turned out to be not that far from our house. However, in Spain, a TomTom is often of no use, and I'd discovered that I couldn't rely on a Google Maps pin, as I'd been stranded more than once on a steep goat path where turning around was impossible. I had to reverse down the mountain with sweat coating my back that time. Fortunately, this time the journey was easier.

I drove through the village, following directions onto a road leading into the valley, a place I had never visited before. It was noticeably greener than our own mountain. When the navigation announced my arrival at the destination, I had to do a double take. It hardly resembled the beautiful spiritual centre I had imagined. Instead, I found myself looking at a dilapidated house, flanked by an iron fence. Was this really the right place? I got out of the car, noticed an intercom by the gate, and pressed the bell. To my relief, I heard Camm's voice, and the rusted gate creaked into motion. Once opened, it revealed a gravel lane. I followed it and drove past several old, dilapidated houses, which made me seriously wonder where I had ended up. Knowing Sander was here was reassuring, though; otherwise, I'm not sure I would have proceeded through the gate.

Suddenly, the lane took a sharp left turn, and what I saw next was beyond anything I could have ever imagined. To my left, a steep mountainside loomed so close that my car nearly scraped against it, while to my right, a precipice yawned ominously beside the road. I maintained my composure by focusing straight ahead, which, surprisingly, was no hardship. I felt as if I had driven straight into paradise. The precipice opened up into a valley, revealing a river and a waterfall, as well as the ivy-covered opposite mountainside. I felt as though I had stepped into an Indiana Jones movie.

The road widened, and several small wooden cabins appeared on the left. To the right, there was a large green expanse featuring an outdoor kitchen, a terrace, and a pool overlooking a yoga platform.

As I parked the car, I could already see Sander walking toward me. Sporting a bare torso, a work belt, and a few weeks' worth of beard, he looked like a cross between a caveman and George Clooney. He looked great!

After parking the car and double-checking my handbrake, I got out and embraced him in a heartfelt hug. It felt surreal to reunite with him in Spain once again.

He assisted with my bags and led the way to a spacious terrace shaded by a bamboo roof. At its centre, an array of delicious dishes adorned a lengthy table. A group of volunteers were enjoying lunch. A petite, red-haired woman stood up and was evidently the yogini of the group. This was Camm, who immediately welcomed me with a hug and a kiss. She then introduced me to her husband, Michael, a tall man adorned with tattoos and sporting a polished bald head.

    She invited me to join them for lunch, and before I knew it, I was deeply engaged in conversation with the colourful individuals around the table. The volunteers and guests, hailing from various nationalities and backgrounds, had a rich tapestry of stories to share. It was only as the sun set that I realized how much time we had spent engrossed in conversation. Using the flashlight on my phone, I made my way to my cabin. This small house, constructed entirely of wood, offered a cozy retreat. Camm and Michael had given each cabin a distinctive appearance. They had crafted by hand beautiful patterns and drawings on the walls, infusing each space with creativity and warmth. They used natural materials, including bamboo tables and chairs, to make the furnishings, and they decorated the bathroom with natural stone and a handmade mosaic. That night, I slept soundly and peacefully.

The next morning, the dull thuds of hammers striking heavy logs of wood woke me, accompanied by the sound of people talking and laughing. It was still early; my alarm clock showed six o'clock. Here in Spain, starting work early in the morning made sense, as by noon it would become too hot to do much else. I quickly put on a dress, made my way to the common dining area, and helped myself to a plate of oatmeal with fruit from the buffet.

    Holding my plate, I walked toward the source of the sound. Next to the pool, a balustrade offered a prime spot to watch all the activity. Looking down, I saw a vast concrete area, about the size of a tennis court, strewn with bamboo stalks. A group of men were endeavoring to lift a mega-sized bamboo pole onto another. Their tense muscles and bare upper bodies shone in the morning sunlight as they hoisted the massive trunk high above their heads. I had never witnessed a scene like that before, especially while having breakfast.

The pole the men were manoeuvring was part of an enormous roof constructed from bamboo. Curved bamboo stalks were attached to this structure, artfully arranged into the shape of large leaves, which together resembled an immense mandala flower. This architectural marvel would cast shade over what would soon be a yoga platform; the very floor where I would create a work of art. The area spanned at least twenty by thirty metres!

I looked at the floor in disbelief, and then it dawned on me that this assignment might take longer than three days. Be careful what you wish for, I thought. You wanted to create a great work of art? Well, here you have it!
    I spent the following days sketching. I tried to get more and more in touch with the place and the people, so that intuitively a drawing might emerge. It was day three when I had a sketch that I felt was right.
    It was time to put my ideas to the test. That morning, Camm kindly provided some crayons for me. As I approached, I noticed the men clearing the last pieces of bamboo from the yoga floor.
    Michael and his team then headed towards the forest, where they spent the day planting fruit trees. This left me free to begin my drawing.

Confronted by a six hundred square foot expanse of concrete, I felt daunted. Where should I start? Its vastness made me realise I had to transfer my sketch to the floor, largely by intuition.

I made my way to the two thick tree trunks positioned precisely at the centre of the floor, anchoring the bamboo structure. With a piece of chalk in hand, I began by drawing the first circle around a trunk, and soon, a second circle took shape. Before long, I found myself fully engrossed in the rhythm of sketching, only pausing to look and feel, before continuing with my drawing. Occasionally, I would dip a sponge into a bowl of water to erase any lines that were too crooked, or out of place.

After about two hours, the sun began to warmly kiss my skin, though it was still early in the morning. My tiny top and thin yoga pants felt like too much as they clung to my sweaty body. I moved across the floor with dance-like steps, drawing large circles with my crayon, stretching my arms to their limits to ensure the lines flowed smoothly. The work was intense; sweat streamed down my body. After three hours of diligent effort, I walked to the railing to view the drawing from above and felt a wave of satisfaction. Wow! The magnitude of the work was overwhelming, yet incredibly fulfilling. But the energy was just right, and the drawing brought a perfect balance to this space and its surroundings.

As I stood there, basking in the satisfaction of my work, I suddenly felt a drop on my arm, followed by another, and then another... Surprised, I looked up. Rain?

"It never rains here!" I exclaimed, but no sooner had the words left my mouth than a tropical downpour unleashed itself. My work was obliterated in minutes. I stood there, gaping in disbelief at this sudden act of nature.

Graham, the Swedish pilot who had been assisting with the bamboo project, dashed through the rain toward me and urgently tugged at my arm, leading me to the covered area where everyone else had sought refuge from the downpour.

"Nothing is permanent," Michael remarked, chuckling as I approached, dripping wet.

I was so frustrated I could have strangled him for that spiritual one-liner! 'Nothing is permanent?' That was three hours of intense labour, all for nothing! Yet, Michael remained unfazed by my glare and confidently reassured me that the drawing would turn out even better next time. Deep down, I knew he was probably right, but I wasn't ready to admit it after all that effort had seemingly gone to waste. The rain persisted throughout the day, and after spending the entire afternoon together, by dinner time everyone had had their fill of the weather, so they retreated early to their sleeping quarters. I, too, made my way to my cabin tucked away in a corner of the camp.

After a long, refreshing cold shower, I climbed into bed early. I decided to engage with another meditation, as meditations had become a significant source of inspiration for me. I added it to my playlist and plugged in my earphones.

Recently, I'd been harbouring a profound desire to deepen my connections: with myself, with others, and perhaps even with other dimensions. But I wanted to explore these connections in the tangible realm of reality, rather than through meditation. How would it feel to experiment with this while fully present, not lost in a meditative trance? How could I integrate this heightened level of engagement into my daily life? And then, what would this mean for my relationships with others?

   I experienced a peculiar tension in my body as I formed my intention.

Be careful what you wish for.

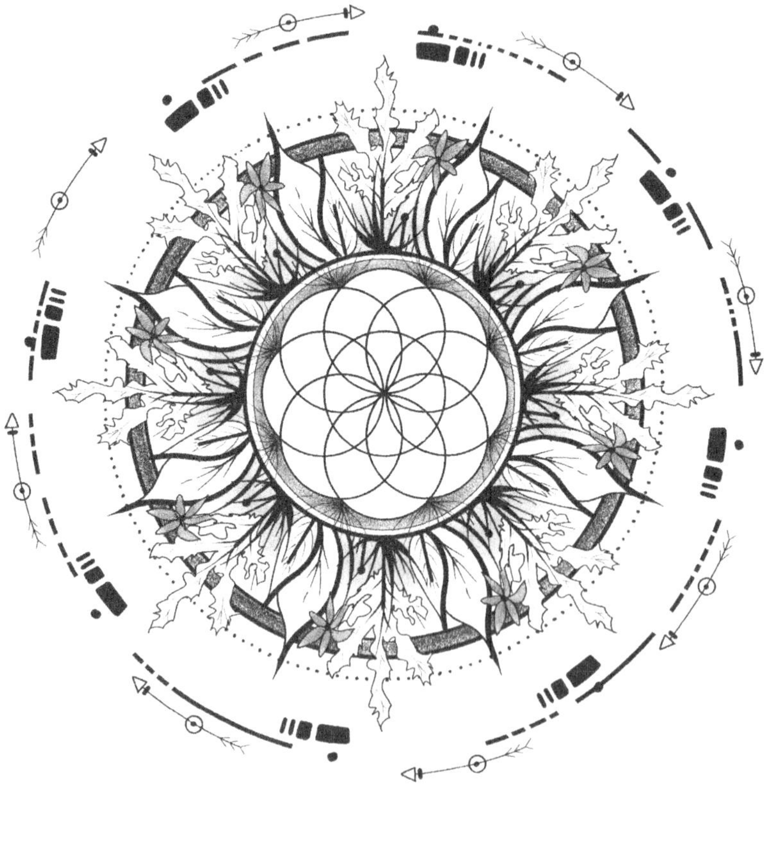

Chapter 10
Sex As A Path To The Divine

After successfully transferring the second sketch more precisely onto the yoga floor, I embarked on the lengthy process of painting. Day after day, I laboured over this gigantic canvas, adopting various positions–sitting, lying down, standing bent over, or crouching–with a paint can in one hand and a brush in the other. I meticulously filled in the chalk lines on the floor with a deep purple hue. Progress was gradual and as I worked, the scorching summer sun bronzed my shoulders to a dark brown, mirroring the complexions of the men who had been constructing the bamboo ceiling for weeks.

Before I realised it, over two weeks had passed. Throughout this time, I lived in sync with the community's rhythm: sharing meals, engaging in conversations after a long day of physical labour, and making new acquaintances. This magical place, thanks to its warm and creative owners, possessed an irresistible allure for the most remarkable individuals. These included both volunteers and guests who arrived for a retreat. For instance, after Sander departed, our group welcomed Stefan, a former advertising executive who had become incredibly wealthy, then spent years on a mountain in Tibet; Graham, a pilot who had recently completed yoga training and was pondering his next steps; Margot, who was recovering from a life-threatening illness and learning to trust her body once more; and a woman who had served in the U.S. Army, operating drones to drop bombs in distant lands, now striving to come to terms with her traumas. Each of us had stepped away from our previous lives on a quest to find ourselves. In pursuing this, we discovered a shared yearning for greater authenticity in our lives.

That evening, after enjoying another delightful meal, a small group of us lingered at the table: Michael, Graham, and myself. As Camm tidied up by washing the last of the cups, we leisurely sipped our coffee, and our conversation naturally drifted towards the subject of humanity.

We discussed the boundless potential humans possess if we could only live from our true essence once more. Fired up by this topic, I shared my experience with Elske, detailing how, together, we had created something beyond what either of us could have achieved individually.

Michael reacted to this enthusiastically, discussing how the world could look vastly different if we began to truly leverage our unique talents. He shared his vision of the future, encompassing living, working, and housing. The topic clearly captivated Graham, who elaborated on his belief that technology could be far more advanced than it is today, potentially bringing us closer to nature. According to him, cars could have been running on water a long time ago, free energy could be a commonplace reality, and living off the grid could be the norm for everyone, thus freeing us from the need to toil relentlessly just to sustain our existence. This man spoke with passion about ideas that, until now, I had only sensed intuitively.

"Yes, exactly!" I wanted to shout out after every sentence. What if, in the world, we were concerned with more than just making money, securing profit, and making short-term decisions purely for personal and financial gain? Imagine if our driving force was precisely that which would truly serve us as humanity, and if we began to truly live again? To enjoy, play, and discover?

All four of us were fully engaged while discussing it. The energy rose with each passing minute, and ideas flowed freely. It felt as though the evening might never end, and in this surge of energy, anything seemed possible. I could sense our deep connection to one another in that moment, realizing that we were sharing not from our egos, but from a place of profound 'knowing.'

Happiness surged through me, serving as a profound sign that when we are truly open to each other and have the courage to connect, incredible things can occur; things we currently deem impossible. By coming together, leveraging our unique talents and wisdom, we can create and accomplish extraordinarily beautiful things.

This feeling was indescribable; it was as though the conversation was almost unnecessary. We knew exactly what we meant and envisioned how that prospect could become a reality. Hours passed, and it was only when we had all become a feast for mosquitoes that Camm and Michael retired to their cabin, leaving me alone with Graham.

Graham mused aloud whether that vision could ever materialise, whether we would live to see such a world. I didn't have an answer. All I felt was a deep-seated knowledge that we all, in some way, already understand this truth, but simply need to be reminded of it. That if we embraced this realisation once more, a significant change could happen in just a day.

Graham immediately grasped what I was saying and affirmed that he felt the same way. As he spoke, I realised words were becoming unnecessary, as our energy intensified with each passing minute. Our conversation meandered through topics, such as other dimensions and our personal explorations of them. It was incredibly reassuring to find someone who not only shared these experiences, but approached them with equal curiosity and without scepticism. He shared countless stories of how he experimented with these concepts during meditation and his journey to understanding their application in our world. My excitement bubbled over as I shared my experience of feeling unified with everything in a supermarket: an experience I had never shared with anyone before, aware of how outlandish it might seem. But Graham immediately became intrigued and bombarded me with questions: 'How did you get there? How did it feel? And what could we do with all that?'

As we continued our enthusiastic conversation, I felt the energy between us intensify. It was as though our surroundings transformed, enveloped in a promise of something more. The space around us seemed to illuminate.

Then, a profound silence ensued; we had exhausted our words. His bright blue eyes locked onto mine, unyielding. In that moment, I experienced an energy similar to what I had felt during my recent meditations; a serene vibration, an essence of being. This sensation was thrilling, imbuing our connection with a profound intimacy. Above all, my curiosity was peaked, wondering what possibilities might unfold if we dared to stay fully present in this moment. I could tell he was contemplating the same.

Silently, we both said YES to something whose exact nature we did not yet know. The tension in the air transformed into a dimension of its own.
   He did not pull away; instead, I sensed his unwavering presence. His steadfastness inspired me to remain as well, to open myself up to more, to yearn for his touch. As if reading my thoughts, he drew me close and kissed me with an intensity that sent shockwaves through my entire being.
   I felt not just my body, but my entire energy field, resonate in the space around us. We connected on an entirely different level.

This was a connection that transcended physical form,
I felt everything:
him, myself, the world,

when I touched him, it was an authentic touch,
I saw him without using my eyes.

He took my hand and led me to his cabin. As we entered, he closed the door behind us, leaving us bathed in the light of the full moon. Looking at him, I understood: this was to be a true exploration, a shared journey into infinite possibilities.

As he gently kissed my neck, it wasn't just his lips but his entire being that seemed to embrace me.

Tears flowed, full of emotion.
At last, I meet you.
Here you are.
Here I am.

I experienced a sense of coming home that transcended the physical realm of stones and gateways. It was a homecoming to a world I always knew existed but had not fully embraced. Our connection spanned the depths of my being, reaching the deepest galaxies. As I touched and saw him, it felt as though he had always been there, as if I had rediscovered him once again. My body trembled uncontrollably, overwhelmed with emotion, as tears of joy streamed down my cheeks.

The energy pulsed, pulsed, pulsed.
   I yearned to surrender to it completely. We vanished, diving through deeper dimensions into a void where everything existed. I felt everything: every hair on his arm, every touch of his hands, every muscle moving under his sun-kissed skin. I was so incredibly charged; it felt as though I could power the entire country.

Every touch was nearly overwhelming; an intense vibration coursed through my entire body. Through the touch of his hands, I experienced myself as if floating a metre above my body. I yearned to feel him even more deeply, to sense the power moving beneath my hands, to feel the surge of his primal energy. My thoughts were completely silenced; I was in solitude with the experience. This dance was of infinite proportions, leading us together into a realm that transcended time and place, demanding nothing but total immersion in feeling and being.

Our bodies seemed to merge naturally, with the energy pulsing more strongly than the mere material of our flesh, erasing any sense of a boundary between us. We became one, and the energy surged, far more powerful than any energy fields I had imagined possible. Our union generated an energy that propelled us into the realm of everything and nothing far quicker than we could have achieved individually.

    His masculine energy enveloped my feminine essence; I could do nothing but surrender. I felt a new aspect of womanhood awaken within me, one I had never encountered before. A sensation of invincibility swept over me, empowering me to take the lead. I embraced this new identity fully.

The gypsy, the dancer, and the sensual woman within me sprang to life. I became a goddess, fully in command, engaging with the man beneath me as though I were charging into battle astride my steed. His strength grew increasingly intense, as if I had created a space for a power he would never have dared to exhibit otherwise. I didn't just invite him; I summoned him, yearning to see him in his entirety, as a man embodying raw, animalistic desire. I wanted him to abandon all restraint, to stand resolutely in his power and dare to gaze deeply into my eyes as he penetrated me deeper and deeper.

    I transcended my body; I yearned to feel everything, truly everything, in that moment. All boundaries vanished, giving way to a presence that was all-encompassing. Love flowed in and out of every pore; my heart opened wider, and tears streamed down my cheeks anew. It touched me at a depth that was unparalleled; I felt myself, him, everyone in the universe, and I took a full sip. And another. And one more. Then another.

Time had vanished, and hours later, the energy gently subsided. We both returned to the reality of earth and fell asleep in each other's embrace. Exhaustion overcame our bodies, yet our souls were enriched–by each other and by the world.

The next morning, I rose with swirling energies under my feet. My body tingled all over, pulsing with life. I felt fuzzy yet present, calm yet tired, my muscles aching as if I had run a marathon the night before. Yet, a peaceful feeling dominated. I wandered through an unfamiliar room that overlooked a mountainous landscape revealing Andalusia in all its glory. The sun was slowly rising over the mountains, casting a purple-pink glow on their peaks. All I desired was simply to be. To be present here, nothing more.

I hadn't noticed Graham getting out of bed, but suddenly I heard his voice softly in my ear, "Can I make you a coffee, beautiful?"

I felt his warm body against my back, and the energy in my belly flared up instantly.

"Yes, that would be delicious," I responded as I turned and wrapped my arms around his neck.

His eyes didn't just look; they explored. His gaze told me he wanted to know more. I smiled. Who was this man who had so suddenly entered my life?

As I basked in the warmth of the rising sun at my back, our eyes remained locked in a togetherness neither of us wished to break. Then, he bowed his head, and his lips once again found their way to that spot on my neck. I wanted to forget everything; my only desire was to embark on adventures to unknown worlds with this man. In complete surrender, I gave myself to him once more.

After that, I yearned to return to the present moment. I got out of bed and stepped into the shower. The sensation of water cascading over my body was soothing.

However, this tranquility soon gave way to a wave of sadness, as I felt a profound sense of intense loneliness. After experiencing the euphoria of feeling truly 'home' and deeply connected, I was now confronted with the other side of the coin. A sudden, profound realisation of what I had missed in my life for too long struck me. Grief surged in my throat, my body tensed, and tears streamed down my cheeks, as a sensation akin to a tightening belt enveloped my heart.

This was the other side of what I had so deeply longed for. 'Be careful what you wish for' suddenly rang true: with every desire comes its downside. This was that wave, that inevitable movement that arises when you surrender to everything, when you dare to relinquish control. And so, I entered the valley of the wave.

Physical exhaustion gave my mind the space to wander into all kinds of thoughts. How foolish it all was to have let myself go to such an extent. 'This is what happens when you relinquish control over everything: you end up sad in a shower!' One critical thought after another berated me, each laden with reproaches about my reckless behaviour. It was a dangerous path; I couldn't afford to let everything go.

Too exhausted to resist these thoughts, I let my Swedish pilot continue sleeping as I quietly slipped away to my cabin.

Despite the turmoil of dark thoughts and heavy emotions, my experience with Graham remained the most beautiful I'd ever had. And no matter how fervently my mind attempted to draw me back to the familiarity and security of my old reality, I knew one thing for certain: there was no turning back.

I had discovered the true essence of what a relationship could be. The immense power between a man and a woman in complete surrender. How I found my way back to this energy and dimension, this intensely beautiful experience, has been indelibly etched into my cells, making the memory more potent than anything else.

So, I accepted the downside as a given. The panic attacks were permitted to be present, but I reassured my body: this is safe, this is where we can truly be ourselves. This was the gateway to the infinite world I had always known existed.

There, I could reconnect with the source, with myself, and feel life pulsating through my veins. Yes, despite everything, YES! This is what I wanted.

The next day marked our last day together in southern Spain, as it was the day Graham would return to Sweden. Uncertain if our paths would cross again, I found solace in the completeness of our encounter. It had fulfilled its purpose. As we bid farewell to everyone, he embraced me tightly one last time. Our eyes locked, conveying an unspoken recognition of the profound experience we had shared.

"'I will never forget this," he whispered, holding me close. "We are connected forever."

Chapter 11
Creating Without Thinking

The surge of sexual energy appeared to fuel my creative power directly, as suddenly my inspiration became unstoppable. That weekend, I worked tirelessly, not just on the yoga floor but also on paper, sketching several new mandala designs simultaneously. The ideas flowed so freely from my pencil that I could barely keep up.

Looking at a just-drawn mandala design lying in front of me on the table, I thought: 'Actually, I would like this on a T-shirt.'

No sooner had the thought crossed my mind than I grabbed a black shirt from my closet, took out white paint, thinned it with water, and dipped a thin brush into it. With a steady hand, I drew fine lines and shapes on the cotton.

After half an hour of painting, I held up the T-shirt. The mandala design looked like a painting on it, and it looked super cool! I was absolutely thrilled. 'Could I get this printed?' I wondered. The idea of having my own designs on T-shirts excited me immensely.

I sent some pictures to a designer friend, asking for his opinion. He was immediately excited and requested one of the pencil drawings.

Just an hour later, I received a digital file from him. Without delay, I found an online company that could print this file on T-shirts and straight away ordered a few test copies.

While I was putting the finishing touches on the yoga floor, I realized I had been at work for about three weeks. On the last morning, I looked down from the railing above at the yoga floor, now adorned with the huge artwork. The paint, glistening in the morning sun, signaled that my creation was ready to welcome the first sun salutations.

Camm and Michael were immensely pleased with the artwork on their yoga floor. They invited me to stay longer and participate in the community. Although the idea of living with a group of like-minded people was appealing, something inside me felt that this wasn't the right place for me. It was time to leave.

A few days later, back at my sister's finca, the newly printed T-shirts arrived. That afternoon, my sister played the role of a model. She showcased the T-shirts with the flair of Naomi Campbell while I took photos. Using these photos and the story behind the designs, I constructed the first pages of my own online shop. Fortunately, my background in web development came in handy. My marketing experience turned out to be valuable after all! I posted the first T-shirts on Facebook the same weekend and saw the first orders come in that very day.

A week later, my sister looked at me with pride. "You manifested that cleverly, sis! You go off to paint a yoga floor for a few weeks and return as a clothing designer."
    Indeed, I hadn't seen that coming myself. Perhaps that's why it felt so right and unfolded so effortlessly. My mind hadn't interfered at all. I hadn't planned any of this; it had all sprung from pure inspiration in the moment.

That month, I sold hundreds of shirts. I created two more new designs and noticed people making repeat purchases after their initial one. I was utterly astonished by this success.

It was remarkable how everything had come together. This is how I wanted to live, this is how I wanted to work: creating from inspiration, not forcing anything, simply flowing with what emerged.

How did that work in practice? I had no idea. I sensed that this approach to business was a major departure from what I was familiar with. No control, no security–just moving along with whatever happened. Nothing solid to hold on to, nothing to grip.

I had truly experienced that when I didn't cling to control, when I let go and dared to surrender, that's when the real magic happened. In those moments, I created things beyond my wildest dreams.

This flow of creation was what I wanted to empower. During my next meditation, I knew exactly what I wanted to experience.

No more control.
Living in the moment.
Riding the wave of life.
Letting the magic unfold.

Chapter 12
Intuition Is Richly Rewarded

I committed to letting everything arise in the moment, yet part of me believed I could subtly influence the outcome. I imagined that what would naturally emerge could be exciting art projects or perhaps a gallery eager to sell my artwork for thousands of dollars.

However, the intention I had set during my meditations focused on working in the flow, creating in the now, and surrendering to whatever wanted to emerge. So, I was completely taken aback by a question I received out of the blue a few weeks later from a close friend. Caroline was on the phone, passionately discussing her mission of helping people to embrace life fearlessly again. It resonated deeply with me; it was exactly what I believed the world needed. But then, she posed a question that I hadn't anticipated.

Create a website? Startled, I declined three times, loudly enough for Caroline to understand my absolute reluctance. Panic surged through me. True, I had built an online shop for myself and was proficient at it, but I had vowed never to engage in that work again. Despite my repeated refusals over the phone, something peculiar happened: deep down, I actually felt a 'YES.'

This reaction surprised me, but having known Caroline for a while, I could articulate what was happening: I actually felt a 'YES' to her question, but panic ensued because I didn't want to revert to my old job. Caroline remained calm and, with pinpoint accuracy, touched upon the core issue by asking what that old work represented to me.

I immediately recognised the feeling. It was about engaging in tasks I didn't want to do but felt obligated to because there was payment involved. This put me in the unequal relationship of client and web designer, where I sensed my freedom slipping away.

Freedom – that was the crux. Caroline, with her astute insight, suggested exploring a completely new way of working. "What if you could work in total freedom? What would that look like for you?" she asked.

I paused for a moment, striving to distance myself from the panic-stricken attempts of my mind to seize control, and instead focused purely on what mattered to me. Hesitantly, I articulated my thoughts. "Okay, if I'm going to build a website for you, it has to align with my current approach to life." I brainstormed aloud, not in search of an answer, but to clarify my own thoughts.

"I need space," I continued. "The freedom to create your website in the same intuitive manner as I approach my painting. This means truly connecting with you and your work, allowing what needs to emerge naturally. No predefined plans or strategies!"

"Good, let's do that!" Caroline said enthusiastically. "I trust your intuition and creative power completely; you have carte blanche with no reservations."

"Okay, but let's approach this as an experiment," I responded, still with a hint of caution. "If it doesn't work out, then it doesn't work out."

"Absolutely!" Caroline agreed.

I could sense Caroline's confidence over the phone; I was the only one who needed to be convinced.

That afternoon, I allowed the idea to fully percolate. Gradually, I started feeling excited. Caroline aimed to make the world a better place, driven by her own inspiration. Just last month, we had spent evenings discussing how wonderful it would be if everyone pursued their passions in this way. Now, I had the opportunity to support someone like her in gaining visibility, empowering her to communicate her mission effectively and create a measurable impact. Wasn't this precisely what I had always wanted?

My mind sought clarity, yearning to understand how I could meld this with my art. Was I an artist, a writer, or a web designer now? However, I didn't dwell on these questions for long. They were relics of an older mindset. In this new way of living, traditional job titles were irrelevant. It no longer mattered if my LinkedIn headline didn't fit neatly into conventional categories. What I truly sought was to break free from all those labels, to live and work with freedom. I realized I didn't have to confine myself to a single role; I was free to simply be myself and let that authenticity guide my path.

That week, Caroline and I had our first phone session. Me in Spain, her in the Netherlands, both of us united by the same goal: to create a website that embodied everything about Caroline; her essence interwoven through every line of code. Unlike my previous approach of drafting a marketing plan and structuring the website development, I let go of all that. The phone call proved to be an exceptionally effective way to delve into the project. Wanting to understand and feel her motivations, mission, and dreams, I listened, but more importantly, I connected with her on a deeper level through our conversation until I could sense her purpose and her mission in the world.
When, after about an hour of brainstorming, I suddenly felt goosebumps, I knew we had reached the core of what mattered. Her story deeply moved me, and I felt like I was finally seeing her true essence. Caroline became emotional, surprised by this revelation about herself. Having truly seen her, the ideas started flowing rapidly. Colours, words, and images surfaced effortlessly, and I hastily noted each one. I could envision the entire website so vividly that I promptly ended the call, eager to bring this vision to life in the online

world.

Building the site was akin to painting. I laid out the initial blocks, images, and text. I observed and felt what was right and what needed adjustment, then went back to refine it. This natural creative process led to a promising first draft of the homepage within a week.

   I sent the draft to Caroline and quickly received an enthusiastic response.

   'Tessa, it's as if you could see inside my head!' she wrote. 'I'm going to take a closer look over the weekend, but my first impression is fantastic.'

This experiment utterly captivated me, and my work on the website seemed to unfold naturally. This approach felt effortless and perfectly suited to me.

   For years, I believed that working from a place of freedom and intuition was impossible in a commercial environment, which led me to abandon my marketing and web design endeavours. I had convinced myself that true creative freedom, and the ability to be authentically myself, was only possible within the confines of the art world.

   The freedom I embraced in this experiment proved to be the key. It was not confined to the creative process alone, but extended throughout our collaboration. I had the option to withdraw at any moment, and similarly, if the work did not resonate with her, she was free to stop with no financial obligation. I would have never considered taking such a risk in the past, but now I embraced it willingly. This autonomy was paramount. It was the condition that allowed me to create freely, being fully open to whatever emerged. It provided my intuition with the space it needed to guide me.

Two months later, when we completed the new website, another client came forward unexpectedly. Through this initial experiment, I discovered exactly how I wanted to work. Freedom, equality, and genuine curiosity from both sides were vitally important, and I made a promise to myself to always stay true to these values.

Each client led to another, all without any need for me to advertise. Work came consistently, always arriving at just the right moment. I worked on these projects alongside my painting and T-shirt designs, feeling truly fulfilled. What started as months of work flowed seamlessly into a year of effortless creativity.

There was only one moment, after dedicating eight hours to a project, when I felt this wasn't going to work. I returned the assignment and chose not to charge for my efforts. In response, the client mentioned how valuable she found our telephone sessions and expressed a desire to continue them. In the months that followed, I naturally attracted new clients for these sessions, marking my spontaneous foray into the business coaching profession.

Entrepreneurship had never felt so natural. Beyond the satisfaction of earning a good income, there was an even greater reward: I had developed a working method that allowed me to remain true to myself, closely in tune with my feelings, and always sincere. This was something I had always believed to be crucial, but had thought impossible to maintain in a business context due to misplaced priorities; security and profit. My experience now affirmed a new deep-seated belief: prioritising connection, following your heart, and trusting your intuition leads to rich rewards!

Chapter 13
Stoking The Inner Fire

Sometimes, my mind still tried to categorise my roles: I was now an artist, clothing designer, entrepreneurial coach, and web designer. My inner controller craved a grip, finding it challenging to manage so many roles simultaneously. However, whenever I sought clarity and focused solely on painting, for instance, I quickly realised that wasn't my true calling. My other talents protested, sending me signals through stomach pains or muscle cramps from excessive painting. My body acted as a direct communication channel from my soul, using undeniable physical discomfort to remind me I was meant to embrace my full potential, not to be confined to a single function or talent. What truly motivated me was not painting, writing, or web design in themselves; seeing people live out their full potential energised me. Sometimes, I could almost taste it, imagining a world where everyone seized their capabilities with both hands. What a brilliant world that would be!

And I wasn't alone in this vision. The more connected I felt to this idea, the more inspiration flowed my way. It was by such serendipity that I stumbled upon a documentary about Michael Reynolds, an architect on a mission and the inventor of Earthships. These are self-sufficient homes designed to provide a family of four with all the essentials: shelter, energy, and food. This concept was precisely what I had been envisioning. Imagine the potential of his discovery! It offered a path to freedom, a way for everyone to live freely.

Unsurprisingly, the documentary revealed how various authorities attempted to block his efforts. After all, it is not so easy to manipulate a free individual, nor is there much you can sell to someone who lacks for nothing. He is truly alive! Yet, he remained undeterred, continuing to gift families the freedom of living in *Earthships.*

This was the world I yearned to be part of! I felt his spirit through my screen. And more so, I realised the supreme importance of fulfilling one's purpose in the world. We each have a unique contribution to make to the collective. When everyone uses their talents in such a manner, we don't just encounter a single genius idea; we become inundated with innovation.

Look at Ricardo Semler, an entrepreneur who made employee happiness his top priority and became the most successful entrepreneur in Brazil. He pursued this path despite scepticism and criticism, guided by a deep conviction that it was the right thing to do.

Such inspiring examples ignited my inner fire. I regularly dedicated time to delve into biographies and documentaries about these visionaries and free thinkers.

These were individuals with the courage to stand by their convictions, even when the rest of the world doubted them. Indeed, these are the kind of people we need more of; the ones who brush aside fear like an annoying gnat and, through their actions, momentarily propel the world forward by leaps and bounds, simply by fulfilling their purpose.

Feeling so clearly that what one must do requires both courage and surrender, accompanied by the realisation that one has no control over how things will unfold, I aspired to work in connection, to create with inspiration, and to contribute to making the world a better place–and I achieved it! However, the journey unfolded in ways far different from what I had initially envisioned.

Could I embrace this unpredictability and flow with it?

Chapter 14
The Monkey Mind

When you try too hard to hold on to something, it often slips right through your fingers. And as is often the case, a valley followed the peak. The flurry of activity came to a sudden halt, and silence ensued. Days of quiet turned into weeks, and before I knew it, an entire month had passed with no developments. One evening, as I opened my laptop to be greeted by an empty calendar, I felt the onset of a panic attack.

The thoughts rattled around in my head. Perhaps I wasn't meant to take this path after all. What was I thinking, trying to follow my intuition? How naïve of me to think this approach was working. The old adage that you must work hard for your money, that it doesn't just arrive effortlessly, seemed to hold true. Maybe returning to my previous marketing job wasn't such a bad idea. After all, there's a reason that field is lucratively compensated by society. What was I doing venturing away from it? It would be far simpler to work a regular job, receive a consistent paycheck, and follow society's norms.

The Monkey Mind was on high alert, a term often used in psychology to describe when your primal brain takes charge. It felt all too fitting, as if a monkey were indeed swinging wildly through my thoughts in sheer panic.

I scanned the multitude of marketing job postings cluttering the internet; anxiety fueling my restlessness. Meditation could have been my sanctuary, yet the thought of sitting still and finding peace was the furthest from my desires. Instead, I compulsively consumed Mars bars, stomped my feet in frustration like a petulant child, and berated myself for not fitting the mold. How I wished I could conform to the system. With my university degree, I could earn substantial sums. What was I doing here, perched on this mountain, pretending to follow my intuition?

I was berating myself and caught in a cycle of over-analysis. Yet, on an energetic level, it appeared I had sent out a distress signal. Despite my aversion to seeking help–to the point of preferring ruin over reaching out–I began receiving messages from people urging me to keep going. Even complete strangers shared how deeply my art moved them, or how my latest blog post had inspired them. If only they could see me right now, I thought.
Nevertheless, their encouragement gradually eased my anger and frustration. It was as if the universe, or someone beyond it, was sending me a message: don't give up, your work is essential.

Eventually, I answered a call from Elske, who had been trying to reach me for the third time in five days. I poured out my frustrations to her, only to discover she had felt the same way that week. Naturally, our conversation turned to blaming the moon phase and solar flares, and within ten minutes, we were laughing heartily at the challenges we were apparently both experiencing.

That afternoon, we decided to spend some time together on a terrace, basking in the sunshine and setting aside our concerns. We enjoyed a glass of wine, each other's company, and the breathtaking view of the Andalusian mountains. I realised that I almost felt guilty for indulging in this moment of pleasure. In the past, such feelings might have prevented me from loosening my grip, even temporarily. But now, I understood the necessity of observing life's flow. Like a wave that reaches a lofty peak and then dips to gather strength, I recognised the importance of taking time to relax and enjoy. Without these moments of reprieve, enduring the long haul would be impossible.

I shared with Elske how the entire ordeal reminded me of a family constellation therapy session I had had shortly after my bankruptcy. At that time, I was devastated, exhausted, and devoid of inspiration, desperately seeking a way to regain my footing and understand how to become functional again. I hoped this therapy, which looks into the dynamics of roles within a family group, would reveal the steps I needed to take and identify the initial actions required for my recovery.

The irony was that I spent the entire afternoon lying on the floor. The facilitator instructed me to rise only when I felt an intrinsic urge to do so, but I felt nothing. According to him, this was precisely the point. He likened my situation to a lion resting on a branch, explaining that a lion remains dormant for 22 hours to conserve energy for when it's truly needed. This period of rest doesn't bother the lion; it understands that conserving strength is crucial for its moment of peak action. The image of that lion has stayed with me ever since.

Yes, I realised that I, too, needed to embrace periods of rest to allow life's rhythms to flow naturally.

Chapter 15
Selling Your Soul

After weeks of silence, I received a call from a lady at a gallery. She was interested in exhibiting my art at their new location in a well-known town just a few mountains away; a town renowned for its villas, none selling for less than two million. She had recently opened a gallery on the town's most expensive main street and was searching for local, up-and-coming artists to add a touch of hipness to the place.

I was absolutely thrilled. Could this be the moment I had been waiting for? Was my art finally going to be recognised? Would this be the validation of my confidence? And was I truly about to make a living from my art?

Right after hanging up the phone, I began selecting the canvases that would mark my debut in the art world. I had been discovered!

In the rush of excitement, I didn't pause to tune into my intuition; I didn't even take a moment to sit down and reflect...

The very next day, I received the contract to sign. Wanting to protect myself, I had my sister review it, and her reaction was far less enthusiastic.

"Do you have to give up fifty percent of the sale if they sell anything?!" she asked, her eyes ablaze with incredulity.

"Yes, sister, that's just how it works in the art world," I attempted to reassure her, and myself. "Otherwise, I'll never make it!" I added dramatically.

"But it's half the selling price, and you still have to cover your materials and taxes. So, for a painting you've laboured over for months, which sells for a few thousand, you'll only net a few hundred euros," she quickly calculated.

I had already run those numbers myself, about ten times. Yet, I saw no alternative.

"Maybe I should just paint more efficiently to sell more canvases," I suggested weakly.

My sister said nothing, but her meaningfully raised eyebrows spoke volumes. She clearly disagreed.

Annoyed, I snatched the contract from her, snapped that I had to start somewhere, and marched into my studio.

That same week, I headed to the gallery with about five of my paintings, loading them into my brother-in-law's convertible with the top down. Among these was a piece I had dedicated the past three months to: an intricate canvas adorned with tens of thousands of dots, evoking the sensation of stepping into a spring valley in bloom with thousands of flowers. It was a technique I had never attempted before. This piece, I imagined, would stand out magnificently against the gallery's pristine white walls. Upon arrival at the gallery on the affluent main street, I received a warm reception. The new canvas, *Spring is in the Air,* immediately captivated the gallery owner, and she promptly hung it in a prime location. It truly looked spectacular, gaining an added dimension within the gallery's ambiance. Seeing my work displayed alongside that of established artists filled me with immense pride.

A charming Spanish tapas restaurant was located just across the street from the gallery. I chose a small table there and ordered a coffee. From this vantage point, I could see directly into the gallery, and it was thrilling to observe how people reacted to my paintings. Everyone paused in front of the canvas brimming with dots. Yes, I knew it had a captivating effect when you saw all those paint drops up close. After about half an hour, I noticed a stylishly dressed young woman enter the gallery accompanied by a much older man. She pointed to my painting. The man nodded in agreement, and then they exited the gallery.

The gallery owner saw me sitting on the terrace and came trotting my way.
    "You've sold your painting!" she told me enthusiastically.
    "What?" I almost choked on my coffee, looking at her in surprise.
    "Yes, a Russian couple. They are not so difficult; they simply buy what they want. Congratulations, you've just sold your first painting for 3,000 euros!"
    Seeing new people walking into the gallery, she hurried back to her customers, leaving me in amazement.

I wasn't sure whether to be happy or sad. Of course, it was tremendously cool that my art had sold. But it was also the first time I didn't know where my artwork was going to end up. It was the first instance where the intention behind my canvas, what I was truly painting, would remain unknown to its new owners. I let it sink in for a moment and then walked over to the waitress, asking, "*La cuenta, por favor.*"
    After settling the bill, I headed home. There was work to be done.

The sales didn't stop with that one painting. My art became an outright hit, and I emerged as the best-selling artist of the month. My ego received its full measure of validation: I was seen; I was desired. However, the gallery owner mostly saw dollar signs and began inquiring about new work daily. I tried to explain to her that my paintings developed slowly. After all, I applied the paint to the canvas drop by drop, requiring significant drying time in between, and I worked completely intuitively. It was far from an efficient production process. She urged me to find a way to produce them faster, stressing that being in demand meant seizing the moment.

    I fully embraced her fear of missing out on this opportunity and adjusted my working method accordingly. I selected a single colour palette to paint an entire collection simultaneously, allowing me to work on several paintings at once. Before I knew it, I had filled my workspace with over ten tables, each holding canvases that were drying. I moved from one to another, painting tirelessly. For ten hours a day, I hunched over my work, a practice that quickly started taking its toll on me. The prolonged hours of painting led to severe back pain, and in the mornings, I could hardly get out of bed; a bed that, incidentally, was enveloped in the smell of paint fumes from the canvases. With the summer heat making it too hot to work outside, I worked in my bedroom, a poorly ventilated, dark basement. I lived in sunny Spain but had to buy two daylight lamps so I could work inside. I appreciated the irony!

After a few weeks, my new paintings were essentially complete, which was fortunate since the works I had in the gallery had sold out already. However, one evening, after falling asleep utterly exhausted, I awoke in the middle of the night to palpitations. Despite the fan running at full speed, sweat streamed down my back, and I felt waves of anxiety coursing through my body.

'Was I having a heart attack?'
I thought I was dying. 'What am I doing here?
I want control back.'

My ego and Monkey Mind were back in full force, tightening their grip significantly. But I knew how to handle this panic: I needed to focus on the fear rising in my gut.

'Recover. Come on, just keep breathing.'

I knew I had to breathe deeply into my belly, to make contact with the fear there and invite it to grow even bigger. For a moment, the fear indeed intensified, but then it quickly subsided. Fear, when directly confronted, dissipates. Gradually, I sank back into a restless sleep.

The next day, I brought my new artwork to the gallery. However, I left quickly this time, feeling the pressure to continue working. So, that same afternoon, I started on my next collection of canvases. But the gloom of the basement slowly but surely infiltrated my inner world as well. Despite receiving messages almost daily from the gallery owner–either about a piece of my art selling or to share visitors' enthusiasm for my work–it no longer brought me any genuine happiness.

I realised that the artist's life was becoming increasingly difficult for me; every day was a struggle to make something meaningful. It felt as though the walls were closing in on me. I continued to paint, but the joy that had once fueled my creativity was fading. The flow that had once been effortless was now gone. As I attempted to maintain control, I barely kept my head above water. Within a few months, I had reverted to a very familiar state of 'survival mode.'
    Just getting by, with barely enough work, relaxation that was anything but, and a mind that was constantly overworking. I tried every possible way to regain control of the situation, but it felt as though everything was slipping through my fingers.

One afternoon in my studio, as I looked around at all my works of art and felt the ache in my muscles, the realisation hit me. I had not only lost sight of myself, but I had also become disconnected from my work. The passion had dissipated; the bond with my art had completely receded into the background. In a matter of weeks, I had gone from being a free individual into being a slave to my art, driven solely by the allure of money, the majority of which, incidentally, went to the gallery rather than to me.

I realised I had let myself be seduced, and I suddenly felt the full extent of my entrapment: the pursuit of success, fame and money had led me to willingly place my head in a vice.

 I saw no other choice; I MUST do this, otherwise, I wouldn't earn anything at all. This was the norm for all artists, wasn't it?

I was distraught.
Yet, amidst the turmoil, a clear thought emerged. There was only one path forward for me: surrender, meditate, reconnect with myself, establish a connection. Don't overthink.
 But my mind screamed in protest: don't even consider it! If you stop working now, you'll lose everything again! Of course, you need to think, so you can't just sit around meditating now! Are you out of your mind?

I recognised that voice, trying to deter me from introspection. However, my recent experiences with this alternative lifestyle fortified me this time. I understood the importance of reconnecting with my inner self. Despite feeling extremely restless, I sat down to meditate. Throughout the session, I felt myself opening up, cell by cell. I was coming home to myself, and after thirty minutes, tears streamed down my cheeks. The realisation was crystal clear: I needed to be true to myself. A sense of relaxation swept through my muscles, softening my body. I was present once again. And when I opened my eyes, I clearly understood what was truly important to me now.

Without the need for analysis, I felt with razor-sharp clarity that I needed to leave the gallery. As practical as it was to sell my art there, and as much exposure as it provided, it no longer felt right at this moment in my life. I couldn't articulate why, but I knew it to be true.
 That very day, I removed my art from the gallery. So much for dreams of big money or fame. This path was not nurturing

at all. On the contrary, it had left me feeling drained.

Selling my art through a gallery was, essentially, just a concept; a belief that it was a necessary path to market my art. But, of course, there is never just one way. Could I open myself up to other options? Explore beyond the familiar to discover what else might be possible? This thought reignited my curiosity.

Yes, this was precisely what I had been yearning for, wasn't it? To perceive the world as brimming with possibilities, unconfined by narrow expectations.

Chapter 16
The Money Flow

After my debacle with the gallery, I took a breather. I didn't paint anything for a while, which matched the low energy I felt at that moment. Spain was experiencing a heatwave, so I lay motionless on the couch, flanked by two exhausted dogs, with a fan roaring like an airplane taking off. However, this passive attitude gave me a bit too much time to think about my finances.

With my laptop on my lap, I reviewed my accounts in Excel for the umpteenth time. Lately, I had started selling my paintings again. The sales were reasonable: living with my sister meant I didn't have many expenses, allowing me to make a living from my art. However, I didn't plan to stay there forever. The next steps toward independence were buying a car and then a house of my own. But how was I ever going to achieve that? The money trickled in so slowly. I needed a few thousand euros, but had managed to save just three hundred. Dejected, I closed the laptop, at a loss for words. How was I going to pull this off?

I could review my Excel spreadsheet a hundred times, but a work of art would still be a work of art, and a web design client would remain just that. These numbers wouldn't suddenly multiply by ten. I felt utterly baffled, as if my ability to reason had deserted me. My thoughts were trapped in an endless loop, futilely hoping for a different outcome. Anger surged within me towards a world that seemed oblivious to my existence. This was supposed to be my purpose, wasn't it?

I firmly believed that the right path for me involved creating art, following my instincts, and working intuitively. So why was it so impossible to make a living from it?

Once again, I stared at the tables on my laptop, searching for an outcome that seemed just as elusive as before.

Should I take on more clients to build websites? Or should I approach another gallery? The mere thought tightened the knot in my stomach. No! That was not what I wanted. None of those options felt right.

But then what?
What now?!

"Okay, I give up," I declared dramatically to the universe, or to the void in my living room. Thinking about it all had left me utterly exhausted.

"Bring on that surprising twist!" I added sarcastically.

My sister's head came around the door. "Are you okay in here?" she asked with a challenging smile.

I laughed too. "Yeah sure, just battling with myself for a moment. Let me." She closed the door again.

'You know you can't figure it out,' I thought to myself. 'You know how it works!' I took a seat in front of the fan, not only to cool down but also to blow out all the control mechanisms in my head and send my great desire for a full income into the universe.

I had come to understand the power of energy, hadn't I? I had already manifested so much simply by focusing my thoughts. Yet, it remained a formidable challenge. It wasn't about merely wishing and hoping; it required a deep, unwavering belief. But did I truly believe that I could achieve abundance through my art? Or was there something within me still resisting?

True belief meant embracing the feeling of abundance, as

if my desires were already fulfilled. This was no small feat, considering I was attempting to feel something entirely unfamiliar. I put my imagination and visualisation skills to the test, lacking any real-life experiences to anchor these feelings.

More importantly, it challenged my protective and controlling instincts. Could I really release the reins and stop trying to control everything?

I started another meditation session, aiming to immerse myself in the feeling of abundance. What would life feel like if I weren't perpetually in survival mode? What sensations would accompany looking at a bank account flush enough to buy that car outright? How would I rise each morning? What would my day look like? Imagine the joy of owning my home, being able to rebuild my life exactly as I wished.

Before I realised it, I was wandering through this new life during the meditation, stepping into a future reality that was not yet present, but was being summoned by me. My smile widened with each passing moment. The meditation concluded with a heartfelt expression of gratitude for this envisioned way of life, and tears of joy streamed down my face. Rising, I felt immensely lighter–as if I had shed kilos of weight. Inspired, I called Elske and suggested we meet for a drink.

Less than a week later, I heard my sister shouting from upstairs, "Did you check your bank account?!"

"My account? Why, did you deposit something?" I joked, laughing.

"Well, I didn't, but someone else did, for both you and me," she teased, her face beaming with joy.

I quickly opened my banking app and was astounded by what I saw.

"A donation! From Mom!" I exclaimed.

"Yes, now you can finally buy that car!" my sister replied, her happiness echoing through the house.

In the days that followed, I eagerly shared my experience with anyone willing to listen. 'Can you believe that?' I would conclude each time. But after recounting the story for the umpteenth time, a realisation dawned on me that I kept repeating my doubt:

'I don't believe it!

I don't believe it!'

Despite the evidence right before me, I struggled to accept it. This was really happening in my reality, yet I found it hard to let the truth sink in.

My goodness, if I couldn't believe it now, how could this money have manifested in my life? The reality I was creating seemed to be founded on my disbelief. Even as it unfolded before me, I found it hard to embrace the concept of living effortlessly.

This realisation made me acutely aware of my behaviour. And with that awareness came a decision: I no longer wanted to hold on to this disbelief.

I understood that I needed to meditate more often, to reprogram my thoughts. I would continue until I completely purged this deep-seated disbelief from my system. Despite my initial resistance and my tendency to control, I also noticed that through these new experiences, I was gradually learning to surrender more and more to the unknown. I started to trust in the unfolding of something beautiful, embracing the not-knowing and trusting that something wonderful was on the horizon.

So, I welcomed it daily in my meditations; the feeling of abundance, owning a place of my own, and effortlessly selling my art. The magic didn't take long to manifest again.

This time, the next surprise didn't knock on the door; instead, it landed in my mailbox. An unknown man had sent me a message, inquiring if I could design a coin for him. It was such an unusual request that I initially dismissed it as spam. My cursor lingered over the trash can icon, ready to delete the email, yet something within prompted me to give the message a closer look.

Upon closer inspection, the email indeed seemed legitimate. The man was in the business of minting coins and wanted to have a 'dot collection' designed. My curiosity now ignited, I replied to his email asking for further details. I also wanted to gauge the seriousness of his proposal.

Within an hour, I received a response. The man identified himself as a Dutch entrepreneur who owned a coin minting business, holding licences to produce official currency for various countries worldwide. He was under a tight deadline to launch a new collection: he needed the design completed within two weeks and inquired if I was up for the challenge. Moreover, he offered a sum to purchase the licence for the design outright; an amount that matched the donation I had recently received in my account, just four days prior. What a coincidence!

I didn't hesitate and immediately emailed him back, assuring him I could start sketching right away. Without even waiting for the final design, he transferred the entire sum into my bank account on the same day. Where just a few days earlier I had been despondently looking at my savings of three hundred euros, my balance had now surged by thousands.

But the excitement didn't stop there! The national currency of Palau, a country in Oceania, would soon showcase my artwork. It was going to be an official currency, sought after by collectors from all over the world!

'It's unbelievable!'
No, wait! That thought was now firmly being put through the metaphorical shredder.
I had to consciously dismiss my disbelief several times a day. But, I did believe!

This was how life could seamlessly flow and align with my rhythm, effortlessly, without any need for my forceful intervention or overthinking.
Simply brilliant!

Riding the wave of this newfound movement, a few days later, I met up for coffee with Patrick, a Dutch entrepreneur and friend living nearby. Our conversation spanned a range of topics, including entrepreneurship, the extensive marketing work he had also engaged in, and, naturally, the transition to my true passion…art. I shared with him my aspiration to earn a sustainable living from my art, confessing that I was at a loss about how to achieve this.

"What would you want to charge for a painting?" he asked me.

"Well, I would need to ask for at least five thousand euros per painting," I replied, and immediately, I continued with an apologetic tone, "But then, not everyone could afford a painting."

"No, I should hope not!" he exclaimed. "It's a luxury item, Tessa. Consider all the time you invest in each painting! You paint drop by drop! It's unique and quite rare. It can't be cheap, can it? If you truly want to make your mark and contribute, you must be able to make a living from it, right?"

"Yes, I suppose you have a point there," I admitted reluctantly.

"But does the idea of charging a substantial amount for your work trouble you?" he probed further.

Yes, indeed, I immediately felt a surge of unrest within me. Would I even sell anything at such prices? Would people value my work? I wondered if I needed to establish myself as an artist before commanding such amounts. Yet, charging higher prices might lead people to take my art more seriously. But what if it wasn't good enough? Indeed, setting that price, demanding that amount, was tied to taking my work–and myself–seriously, and I could sense the fear intertwined with that realisation.

"It's time to break this cycle, Tess," Patrick said with conviction. He stood up and walked to the kitchen to brew more coffee, leaving me a moment to ponder his words.

A moment later, he returned, handing me a cappuccino, and without missing a beat, restarted his barrage of questions.

"What does your ideal life look like, exactly?"

"Well, it involves working with the finest materials–like a quality framer, and the best paints and canvases, in a space bathed in light, a place spacious enough to allow me to create large works effortlessly," I explained with a renewed sense of enthusiasm and energy.

"But, you know, that's not even the most crucial aspect. My paintings possess a unique power. I connect with something profound, and then I paint what demands to be brought into existence. It's vital that I create them this way, free from pressure, in absolute freedom. I aim to immerse myself deeper into that energy, to work within it. That requires ample space–both in terms of time and finances."

Oof, my openness took me aback. Did he truly grasp what I was trying to convey?

"Do you still follow me?" I asked, my voice tinged with uncertainty.

"Absolutely! I really sense that your paintings convey something profound, and you truly need to start embracing this and acting on it!" he responded without a moment's hesitation.

His confidence was infectious. Suddenly, I grasped the essence of what mattered most. Was I ready to fully commit to my purpose? By articulating the inspiration behind my art more explicitly, I could help others understand its significance. This, I realised, could be the key to transcending my financial struggles. Invigorated, I drove home, brimming with renewed energy.

The next day, I had just settled myself on the terrace with an iced tea when a message from Patrick came in.

'Tess, I've taken some time to reflect. I believe it's crucial for you to pursue what you're meant to do, and I want to support you in that endeavour.'

His words made me sit up straighter.

Patrick is typing...

With each passing second, my curiosity grew, and I could feel my heart rate climbing.

'I want to purchase one of your paintings for five thousand euros.'

'Huh, really?' I typed back, astonished.

'Yes. But it should be a new canvas, one that you create with the intention of it being valued at 5,000 euros. List it for sale at that price. Either it sells for that amount, or I purchase it. Either way, it's sold.'

'Okay, wow, I need a moment to process this.'

'Don't just sit there in silence; step into this new reality now,' he urged. 'Could you send me an invoice immediately? Because I want to transfer the funds to you right away.

It was a good thing he couldn't see my open mouth. I had just sold a painting for five thousand euros!

All I had to do was create it.

I had never seen such a large sum of money land in my bank account so quickly. For three years, I had been counting every cent, and now I could finally step out of survival mode. With a sufficient buffer in place, I immediately felt the freedom this afforded me. The pressure was off, allowing me to reconnect with my true purpose.

So, this resulted from aligning myself each morning with my greatest desire: to live life to its fullest potential. That's when everything began to shift. How wonderful it is to be able to live and work so authentically, staying true to one's self. I sincerely wish this for all of humanity. I've come to realise how crucial it is for the greater good that I–and indeed, everyone–embrace our unique roles. Serving in a job that stifles me, where I am merely going through the motions, benefits no one. The essence lies in making a genuine contribution and staying focused on our true path without giving way to distractions.

So, every morning, I began with that intention: to move beyond predefined concepts and mental constructs, truly letting go. That same week, I sold three paintings, seemingly out of nowhere. The buyers ranged from individuals who had read my book and followed me for years to those encountering my work for the first time. Wow, I felt as though I was in harmony with everything, allowing everyone to discover me. Clearly, a gallery was not the only avenue for selling my art. It was remarkable how things had started to flow in a completely new direction, simply by opening myself up to other possibilities.

'Could it be that a new home would reveal itself soon?'

Chapter 17
Flourishing In The Not-Knowing

B ut how on earth do you deal with this?" asked Linda. I had called my friend in Holland to catch up and had just told her how I was surrendering to everything, trying to make life happen.

"So it always remains unclear this way!" She sounded almost frustrated.

"Yes," I responded, laughing, "I know! It's extremely difficult."

And it was difficult. When I briefly lost touch with myself again, questions shot through my head like stray projectiles: What are you going to do then? Are you really just going to trust that things will work out without a plan? Without knowing what to do? What if you then feel nothing for a very long time and nothing flows? What will you pay the rent with then?

"That would drive me crazy!" laughed Linda.

"Yes, but this is what it's about," I continued. "Not wanting an answer to the question of HOW."

I conceded that I often wanted answers to how, when, and then what? And that I get frustrated when those answers don't come. But it's not about those answers. It's about living my essence, becoming visible through that which drives me and truly touches me. You can't capture that in a concept or a job profile. Within such a framework, I always sell myself short. I remember how frustrated I used to be about that. It's something I ran into at the office when I was not doing what my soul required of me. I would inwardly boil with anger. Why didn't anyone see what I have to bring? Once, fully frustrated, I even told a client: "You didn't hire me for this stupid marketing job; you hired me for me. For me! So let me be!"

Linda burst out laughing. "I think you left a badly confused man that afternoon."

"Yes, and now I understand what happened. I wasn't yelling at him; I was yelling at myself for not showing what I really had to bring. I marketed myself as a freelance marketer and then I got angry when someone hired me for that. Hilarious!"

"Yes," Linda agreed, "but if you're mega-frustrated and angry, then eventually things happen."

"Sure, that anger is useful. That's where your real desire is. It's as if that anger awakens something in yourself that has been lying dormant there for years."

We still talked endlessly about our years as freelancers, about the assignments, the hard work, and the big money. We reminisced about how we used to go to the sauna every week and book weekends away as if we were going shopping. But we both concluded that, while that had seemed like fun, it ultimately didn't get to the heart of the matter. We realised how, even though it was unclear and unknown, this path to a life that was right was so much more important. And we hung up with the intention of really doing what was intended anyway.

After the conversation, I realized what a process it had already been. Yes, I had decided after my bankruptcy that I really wanted to live. But that did not mean I was suddenly free and happy to live.

My goodness, feeling your desire was one thing, taking your first step toward it was another, and then...
then I just did whatever.

Because I had no idea.
It was uncharted land.
That blank canvas I so longed for turned out to be very white.
No start, no idea.

I wanted things to be different, so I couldn't start thinking in terms of the solutions I had used before.

Regardless of concepts. Sounded nice, didn't it? But then it became chaos, a mess, at first. I only had one way to go, and that was falling flat on my face a lot, just doing it, complete craziness, trying it out.

There were many times when I looked at myself and thought, 'I'm 42, what am I doing sitting here on a mountain in southern Spain?' Powerlessness took over, thoughts like 'my life will never be good again,' and 'oh shit, I've messed everything up in my life,' disturbed my sleep.

But my goodness! I was living life.

Because the next day I also felt again the openness, the rawness, the honesty, the sincerity of it all.
It was flowing, literally, in my body, in my life.

So, there were no rules, no ideas, no tricks. I could let it all go; everything was already good.

Nice phrase by the way, one that you hear a lot: 'everything is already good.'
That meant more than 'do whatever.'
It stood for sincerely feeling that everything is good, without any judgments within myself.

It was about trust, connection, inspiration. When I felt inspired, I would grab my laptop and type half a book on my screen in one day. And then if that stayed put for six months because nothing came after that, that was totally fine.

It was about presence. Could I feel what was right in the moment and just act on it? And then trust that it was exactly what needed to happen?

Could I step into the flow of life that way?

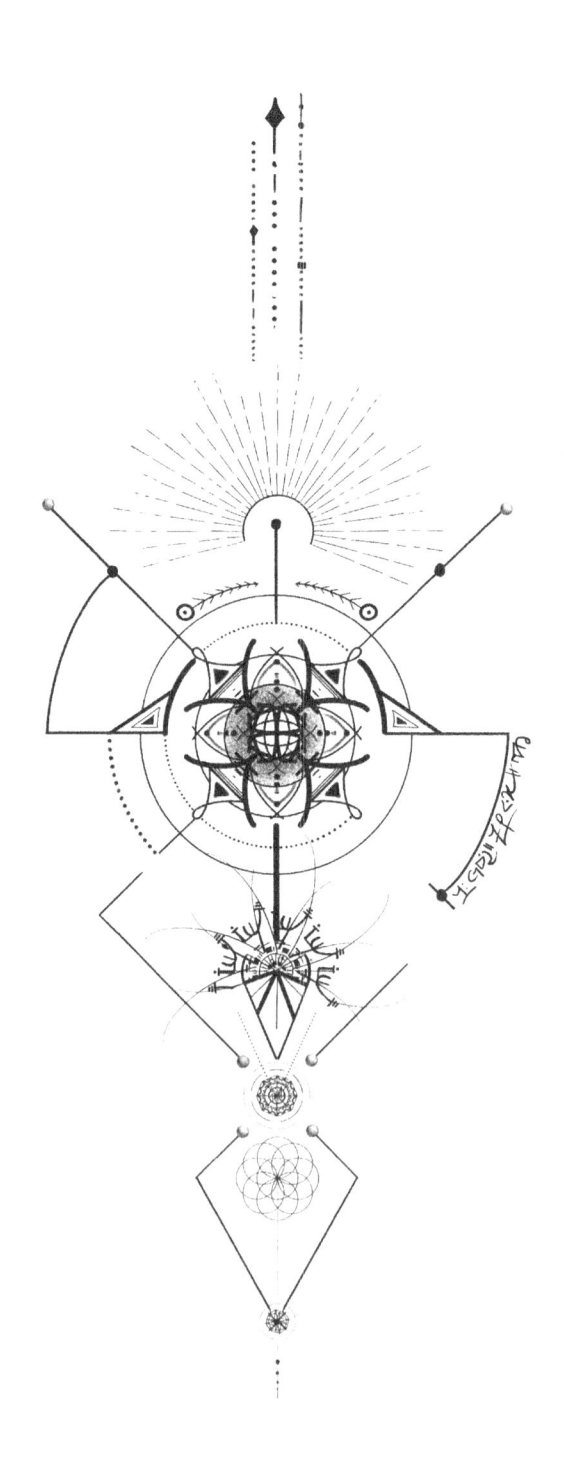

Chapter 18
Working With The Energy Field

Understanding that nothing needed to be framed, and that everything was allowed to be there, it seemed like I had opened all the gates. I felt how great the potential of my art would become if I followed my own path.

Sometimes, I could feel so strongly how wonderful it would be if we all felt who we were again. If we dared to throw off our shackles and be true to ourselves. Start living again! And I knew it was my role to touch this, through my art and through writing. To do this, I had to connect with the energy field of this potential reality as if it were already there.
And create from this connection. When I did that, I felt as if my whole body was activated. A raging river of energy flowed through my veins. Goosebumps accompanied everything I said or did, as if I was completely in touch with life. Everything made sense.

The more I immersed myself in this, the stronger my confidence became. Living and working within this energy made my experiences richer and richer. The number of people I met and connected with grew steadily. I felt a blissful feeling that I couldn't describe.

One evening, I watched a documentary on Bitcoin as the new financial freedom. I could feel this so much! It depicted how we, as humanity, had bound ourselves with the iron-hard restraints of a financial system, and that our only escape was to change it radically. Bitcoin was a beautiful first experiment in this transformation. It is a currency that is not owned by any one country, bank, or person. Instead, it is owned by everyone and exists by the grace of our connection to each other.

I felt so inspired by this virtual currency that I captured its potential and intent in a large Bitcoin painting. The promise was palpably immense. It seemed only logical to put this painting up for sale for one Bitcoin, which at that time was worth about five thousand euros, perfectly aligning with the intention I had set with Patrick. And that decision was validated, because within a day, someone bought the painting and immediately transferred one Bitcoin to me. Suddenly, receiving five thousand euros for a painting was no longer a dream. It just happened, just like that. And I immediately received a commission from another person who was very interested in a Bitcoin artwork.

To make that commission even more challenging, they gave me complete creative freedom; no constraints on size, colours, or the duration of the project. Oh, and he transferred the Bitcoin as payment right away. Once again, I had someone paying me for something I hadn't even created yet!

So much freedom and trust also affected me. There were no concepts or frameworks at all, which is exciting when someone is eagerly waiting for their artwork. The excitement rose even further as Bitcoin's value surged to a staggering 18,000 euros during this process. I had received 18,000 euros for this painting! This thought sometimes almost paralysed my creativity, but this was what I wanted. This was what I longed for–no limiting beliefs, not even about money. So it could be 18,000 euros, but it could also be one euro if the coin collapsed. Was I able to let go of this completely?

I was hugely challenged in terms of trust anyway, because Patrick had already transferred five thousand euros, and he had not yet received a painting for it. Every time I finished a painting, he got to see it first, but so far, his painting wasn't among them. That sometimes made me a little uncomfortable; after all, he had already paid. But Patrick reassured me: "Tessa, I'm not in a hurry. There will be a painting that suits me perfectly. Until then, you just have to create freely."

I sometimes laughed hard at these kinds of brilliant situations, each time receiving exactly what I asked for. And always in a form I hadn't thought of, nicely pushing me out of my comfort zone. But when I dared to go along with that, I was richly rewarded. I now worked in freedom; it flowed. I felt pleasure and curiosity growing. How crazy did I want to make it? Yes, I felt I was far from reaching the limits of my imagination.

And so, each time I experienced both a shortage and mega-abundance of money, it was because it either flowed or it didn't, and the key to that was me.

Chapter 19
You Can't Control It

For the first time, I really enjoyed myself in the Spanish sun. But for the first few months of 2020, I was still restless. I had felt for some time that it was time to take the next step. I had lived with my sister and her husband for five years; it was time to find my own place. Would I stay in Spain or go back to the Netherlands?

I scrolled for hours on Idealista, the Spanish online real estate site, full of beautiful villas. Occasionally, I made an appointment to view one of them. They were truly picturesque houses: fincas overlooking the mountains, each with a private pool, the rental price around 800 euros per month. I knew that in Holland, it was impossible to live like this on this budget. Even so, every time I stood in such a beautiful place, nothing happened. Even in the most beautiful locations, I felt nothing stirring. My body remained anxiously silent, with no enthusiasm, no vision of a life unfolding there. I saw and felt nothing at all.

I actually knew it all along but didn't want to face it yet: I had to go back to the cold, flat Netherlands. During a meditation, when I brought myself back to a sense of being rather than imagining, I literally felt that much more was going to happen in the Netherlands. I even felt that I would meet my future husband there. There was nothing to indicate this, by the way; it was purely a clear knowing, and a strong desire to engage more fully with life. To show myself again. It was time to stop hiding in the mountains of Spain and to step out, to really take up my role in the world.

After that meditation, it was clear. I left the Spanish dream houses behind and turned my attention to the overstressed Dutch housing market. The Dutch equivalent of Idealista would not be of any help, I quickly concluded. I didn't stand a chance in this housing market. No steady income and just back from Spain; two things that would make the average real estate agent think twice. I would not find my place within the system, and of course, it couldn't be more symbolic. Anyway, what did I have to do with these old, rigid structures? There was a whole new world in which much more was possible. It was up to me to open up to it.

Of course, I had wishes: a place in nature, my own home, but with others. I didn't want to be alone in a deserted place. And yes, it needed to be affordable. It felt like an impossible task, but then again, I had tackled those before. To feel how this new reality of a house in the Netherlands would be for me, I assumed the meditation posture once more. I set a clear intention and was curious to see what would happen next.

A few days later, I was talking to one entrepreneur for whom I was building a website, and at the end of our conversation, I mentioned I was moving back to the Netherlands. She immediately became super excited and asked if I already knew where I was going. I told her about my dream home and that I was open to any opportunities that might arise.

    Well, the creation energy did not sit still, because a day later I received a message from her. She knew a lady, Wilma, who ran a small community at a chalet park. She asked if I wanted her to put us in touch with each other.

    As soon as I had her number, I messaged Wilma to see if she had anything available. Less than an hour later, I received an enthusiastic reply that something was available in May– exactly when I had planned to go! She sent me some pictures, and I immediately had a good feeling about it. I asked her if it was okay if a friend came by to have a look. She didn't think that would be a problem.

I immediately called Sander. He had returned to the Netherlands after a year of cycling and thought it would be fun to drop by the park. Two days later, I had an exhilarated Sander on the app. He had made a short video of the place, and I could see from his reaction that he was genuinely impressed.

"You really do get the nicest spot in the park, Tess!" he said enthusiastically, describing what he had seen and how he wanted to live like that himself. Wilma had already shown him several other places. "Maybe I'll become your neighbour here!"

"Really, oh, I'd love that!" I replied happily.

"I'll think about it some more, but your place is a go...yeah, I'd do it."

I emailed back and forth with Wilma some more. What a wonderful flow; this woman trusted her intuition completely and didn't need a contract or deposit. "It's yours. I'll see you in May, and then we'll take care of the rest," she responded when I asked if I could transfer any money in advance.

Wow, exactly the way I used to work myself: just feel it and act accordingly. It seemed to me that Wilma and I were a great match.

What brilliant things were being arranged while I was still in another country! With a big smile on my face, I opened my laptop. That smile soon turned into giggles. I had the first designs of the coin in my mail. How cool they looked! I continued to find it unimaginable that my art appeared on a national coin; a coin that you could actually use in a far, faraway country. Not that people were going to do that; although the coin had a face value of twenty dollars, collectors were likely to buy it for three hundred euros.

"'Do you realise that money is a common thread throughout your story?" asked Linda when we talked again.

"Your first book is about losing all your money. And then you started making money flow paintings."

"Yes indeed, I've also been putting money into paintings," I responded.

"And you live in Coín, which translates to 'coin' in English. You made Bitcoin paintings. And now your art even ends up on a national currency! Really, it's a genius plot twist. How do you dare do all that...just like that?"

"Well, I wasn't that brave, mind you," I said. "I just really had nothing left to lose. It seems I need a crisis every time in order to change again, to get to the point where I really don't know how to go on. Only then do I see room for something new.

"Sometimes, when I look at the world, where one disaster follows another, I think we could all use a good crisis," I philosophised. "We have too much to lose right now, so we are not going to change, even if we feel things are not going in the right direction."

If you sincerely begin to feel that anything can happen... anything! Including the possibility that everything might fall apart or break down, and that you no longer need to possess anything, but can simply be happy in your purest form. Then, space is created for the universe to surprise you with the most magical encounters and situations. This is when that synchronicity arises; the kind that is right, that is true, that gives you goosebumps up to your neck. All you have to do is not interfere!

 You cannot control it. Control does not exist. Not even a little bit.

"What do you mean?" I realised I had lost Linda, so I tried to explain a little better.

"You know, I'm working on my second book. And, as with my art, I want to tell a story. But it's not about me at all. If I truly embrace that, if I accept whatever consequences it may have for me, and let it flow through me, dare to let it happen, then I feel the infinity, the joy. How amazing it is that we get to play in this new reality. I am in this world to tell a beautiful story; one that we all already know but want to feel, hear, and remember again. And the reader engages with my story, because on a subconscious level, they know: I need to feel this, I need to hear this, I need to get activated! I want to live!"

"When everything comes together, I feel extremely connected. Then, I no longer think about where things should go. I feel in the moment what really counts, and then I follow it…"

"Yaaa!" exclaimed Linda enthusiastically. "And in this case, that means you're coming back to the Netherlands. Very cool, this mission of yours, but I am especially happy that my friend is returning. I'm so looking forward to seeing you again in real life!"

"Me too!" I told her.'

We agreed to see each other again soon and hung up.

Yes, it was time to get moving. I had no idea what awaited, but I just felt I had something to do in my home country: the Netherlands.

Chapter 20
Farewell

While on the one hand, I preferred to stay snugly tucked away in a finca on a mountain in Spain, on the other hand, I felt an inner fire ignite. There was an intention for me to rejoin - to go back to the country where I belonged, where I had set so much in motion throughout my life.

I had never really left the party; I had just moved a little further away. And now, I felt like joining the group again, dancing and no longer hiding. It was a very clear desire, a longing for my presence in life.

These kinds of thoughts and feelings regularly caused me to have panic attacks, which made me sit upright in bed at night, or wake up feeling sick to my stomach. Of course, I was not here for nothing. I had felt so free here in Spain: free from judgments, free from participating in the rat race, free from being in a hurry. Would I be able to stay true to myself in the Netherlands? To maintain my rhythm and way of life?

These questions did concern me, but certainly wouldn't change my mind. I had already asked Sander if he was up for a road trip, and he had enthusiastically texted back that he would come to pick me up, and would arrive in Málaga in a few days. I had already started packing the first boxes and bags. Only what could fit in my little Peugeot 207 could come with me, so there was a lot of throwing away and sorting out.

The heat soon made sweat run down my back as I picked

out one box of painting supplies after another. I wanted to bring a basic set, but that still left me with bins of paint. I knew exactly who would genuinely appreciate them.

I loaded the crates of extra paint, an easel, and unused canvases into the car, and drove down the mountain toward nearby Alhaurín el Grande, where I rang Elske's doorbell. When she saw my profile on her intercom, I heard her cheerful voice call out, "Hey, what are you doing here? How nice, I'm coming!"

After a minute, the door swung open. Elske looked at me happily. Then her gaze dropped, and she noticed the boxes of paint. "Wow, are those for me?" she exclaimed happily. But then the meaning of this great gift sank in.

"Oh no, you're leaving!" she said, startled.

"I feel it's time to go," I responded, almost apologetically.

Disappointment was evident on her face. "I knew you'd go. I know you have to, but it feels really shitty."

"I know..." I said, feeling guilty. "Come, I've brought you this peace offering."

"Well, I'm very happy about that!" She was already beaming again. "Oh, all that paint?!"

"You'll get it back when you return, you know!" she laughed, as we walked up the stairs with the heavy crates.

I knew she hoped that would happen, but I also sensed that it would be some time before I would be at her door again.

Once inside her apartment, Elske immediately hurried into the kitchen. When she walked back into the living room with a smile on her face, I saw that she had brought out a bottle of cava and some cheeses.

"Wine?" I took one of the glasses and proposed a toast, "To new adventures"

"To new adventures," Elske replied.

Chapter 21
A New Home

A week later, Sander arrived in Málaga. He spent the first few days acting as a tourist. We visited the retreat centre, ate fish on the beach, and I packed my last bags as efficiently as possible. At the end of the week, the time had come. The car was fully loaded, and we were ready to leave. At three in the morning, we quietly packed our last bags. We had already said goodbye to my sister and my brother-in-law the previous evening, and when we drove off, they were still asleep. I left behind the many works of art I had made here. My sister had promised to send them to me once I was settled in Holland.

As the car growled to life and the headlights illuminated the steep slope of the access road, I swallowed hard. I was leaving my family and this beautiful mountain in Spain, and I felt there was little chance that I would return anytime soon. Tears welled up in my eyes, and I was glad I didn't have to drive for a while. Sander steered the car smoothly up the slope and turned right toward the village. I looked at him for a moment. With the man who had been my faithful friend for over ten years, I was now driving in the dead of night toward a new home in the Netherlands.

Along the way, Sander came up with a delightful surprise.
"Hey Tess, three guesses..." I turned my head quickly and looked at him curiously. I could tell from his voice that he had some really fun news.
"I'm going to be your new neighbour!"

I almost grabbed his neck for a hug, but realised just in time that it might be a little unsafe while he was driving.

"How cool! That will make coming back to Holland so much more fun!"

He laughed at my enthusiasm.

This was indeed a marvellous surprise.

We drove through Spain and France in two days, and in Maastricht, the first town just across the Dutch border, we decided to pamper ourselves with a luxury hotel so that we would be well-rested for the drive to my new hometown Harderwijk the following day. It was wonderful to be back in Holland. Everyone understood me, and I enjoyed a sumptuous breakfast with bread, sprinkles, and cheese.

Then it was time to continue our journey and arrive at my new home.

Chapter 22
A Paradise Of Your Own

And so that morning we headed from Maastricht toward Harderwijk. After leaving the highway, we found ourselves driving along winding roads through the woods. "Wow, how beautiful it is here!" I exclaimed.

"Yes, this is your new habitat," Sander observed, noticing how I was taking it all in.

When we arrived in the fishing village, cyclists almost prevented us from crossing the street.

"It's rather touristy here," Sander commented, sounding somewhat irritated.

"All oldies on bikes. I'll be glad when autumn comes," he continued.

Past the village, we drove toward a forest where, just before the edge of the forest, we turned off onto a gravel path. To the right, we passed a thatched farmhouse, and immediately after that, we arrived at the entrance to the park. We turned into the central area, from where I could see plots with wooden chalets, small houses, and even a camper van. Sander parked the car next to a small shed.

"This is where I live, behind here," he said, pointing. "I'll message Wilma that we're here. In the meantime, I'll show you my cottage."

He walked ahead of me past a tall hedge and opened a small wooden gate. I entered the garden and saw a beautiful, creamy white, L-shaped chalet with a wooden porch on one side and a shed on the other. As Sander opened the door, I looked around the porch. The garden, surrounded by the hedge, offered him a truly beautiful private space–a little paradise of his own.

Even before I could thoroughly admire Sander's cottage, I heard a woman's voice calling, "Hello, good people!"

The gate squeaked open, and Wilma walked into the garden. A woman in her fifties with long blond hair, wearing jeans and a T-shirt, she struck me as a tough cowgirl. With a big smile, she approached me.

"Well, we finally meet!" she said happily, giving me a big hug right away.

I immediately felt a connection with this open and warm woman.

"How was the trip?" she asked.

"I'm glad to be here!" I sighed.

"I get that. Well, shall I show you your home right away then?" Without waiting for an answer, she was already stepping toward my car.

I quickly followed her, and once in the car, she gave me directions as to which paths to take. Sander's cottage was in the centre of the park, but we were now driving toward the side where the forest began. After passing several chalets, we arrived at a cottage with red-green shutters that was partly hidden in a corner of the park.

"This is your new place," Wilma said, as she got out of the car.

I turned off the engine and looked open-mouthed at the little wooden house. It was too cute!

Wilma had to exert some force as she tried to open the cottage's front door.

"The door sticks, because this cottage has been empty for two years," she apologised. "I want to live here myself when my girls have left home, that's why I haven't rented it out until now. Now that I've given your place to Sander, you can live here until another chalet becomes available."

We walked down the hallway to the living room. I was almost blinded by the light. It featured a gigantic glass facade, and the sun was beaming into the room. I felt my heart overflow with happiness. What wonderful energy! The decor was also bright, with a beige sofa and a sand-colored rug on a dark brown wooden floor. A fireplace on the right side already had me envisioning warm winter evenings. To the left, there was a small open kitchen. "It's perfect!" I exclaimed enthusiastically.

Wilma laughed. "Look, it has been untouched for two years. I did a quick clean for you, but you'll have to see past the old stuff, cobwebs, and dust nests."

"I really don't care," I said happily. "The cottage has such wonderful energy!"

"Yes, it's my favourite place, too," Wilma replied.

I had a million questions for her: why had she moved here, how did she manage this park alone as a woman, how had all this had come about? But my fatigue was greater than my curiosity. Wilma noticed that too and quickly said, "We'll talk more over coffee soon, but right now I'm sure you just want to unpack and settle in."

"Yes, very much so," I agreed.

A moment later, Wilma left, and I looked around my new living room. 'I'm home,' I told myself.

The next day I woke up in a new bed, hearing birds singing and trees quietly creaking in the wind. I stepped out of my bed onto the cold floor. Well, the lower temperatures obviously took some getting used to; this was no longer Spain. I walked into my living room and immediately enjoyed the morning sun shining in through the four-metre high glass front. What a luxury! I went to the small kitchenette to make my first cup of coffee. As the coffee dripped slowly through the filter into the pot, I looked outside. To my left was a wooden chalet built entirely of tree trunks. That's where my new neighbour, Wilma's friend, lived. To the right, I looked out over a field of corn. In the distance, I could see the tall treetops of the forest that surrounded the park.

That forest was the first place I wanted to go, to feel the earth under my feet for a while and to breathe in the scent of damp earth. But as I took the last sip of my coffee, I heard a knock at the door and a familiar female voice.

Linda! Five years ago, she had driven me to Spain, and now she was the first to welcome me back to Holland. She always did, by the way. Wherever I moved, she was always on my doorstep in the first week to check out my new home. And with my nomadic existence, that had already taken her all over the Netherlands and even to southern Spain.

I gave her a big hug. "How nice to see you! We have a lot to catch up on again. Would you like a cup of coffee?"

Linda came in with three large plants in her arms and, while looking around, said, "Yes, nice! And where can I put these?"

"Oh, how lovely! Plants for my place; I'm very happy about that."

"How did you get such a great place, anyway?" she asked in amazement.

"I know. I don't know my own powers of manifestation," I replied, laughing. "Again, I didn't see this one coming either. In complete surrender, and this is the result."

"Typical of you," she laughed, as she slumped down on the couch in front of the fireplace. "You always end up in the most beautiful places."

It's true though, I thought as I made the coffee. Regardless of my financial situation, I had always lived in the most beautiful places.

"And what are you going to do here now, then?" asked Linda as she cradled the hot mug of coffee.

"And your painting and your second book?" she continued.'

"I brought some painting supplies, but for now, they're still packed."

"Don't get distracted by the rat race here in Holland, huh? Do keep following your feelings!" Linda told me sternly.

"I'll do my best," I smiled and grabbed her cup and mine for a second cup of coffee.

When Linda had left my new place after an hour or two, I walked into the woods behind my house for the first time. Here I was. Would I manage to keep following my feelings? What was I going to set in motion here? What did it take to fully come into my own here? I didn't have an answer yet. But the fact that my adventure was now shifting into a higher gear had become clear as soon as I got into the car in Spain. Buckle up!

Chapter 23
Dream Start

My home in Harderwijk proved to be enormously calming for me. The forest that began right next to my cottage invited me to take a walk every day, helping me to stay grounded. After all, the transition was significant. I sometimes tried to explain to people the immense difference between the energy in Holland and Spain, but it was hard to put into words. In Spain, the energy moved slowly; this was very nice when you wanted to unwind and slow down by several notches. The country isn't known for its *Mañana, mañana* attitude for nothing.

In Holland, on the other hand, I thundered through the day at dizzying speeds. My goodness, I only had to think of something, and the next day it happened. It was like manifesting on the spot. Consequently, I also had to be careful not to end each evening in something like a feral state, unable to fall asleep because of the adrenaline.

To protect myself, I tried to limit my schedule to one client per day. Creating websites that aligned with the entrepreneur's mission was intense work. Scheduling only one client session a day might sound minimal, but it actually had quite an impact. So, between work sessions, I walked as much as possible in my new forest. It was cool there, which was a relief in the summer. The leaves rustled a relaxing melody, and the gently springy ground under my feet rocked me back into balance, step by step. I felt that returning had affected me deeply. I knew I needed to rest and allow things to sink in. But I also felt the restlessness and uncertainty of building a new life again.

That afternoon, I plopped down on Sander's couch to share a glass of wine. He understood the duality I felt, too. He programmed to provide himself with income, but he really came alive when he was drawing or making music. Despite his passions, he also did not yet dare to take steps into that unknown world. Despite being full of possibilities, that world was so different from what we had been taught. It was nice to have such a good friend living around the corner with whom I could share that inner struggle.

As I walked alone across the park back to my house at the end of the evening, happiness flooded through me. Although I had only been in Holland for just under two weeks, I immediately felt at home again. I enjoyed the sociability of having a friend who lived so close and was happy with the safety I felt walking back to my home along the paths in the evening. I could not have wished for a better situation. It was a dream start to my return. Grateful for this, I made contact with everything around me in the quantum field where I always created these wonderful situations.

Chapter 24
The Power Of Intuition

The next morning, I got up early again. I had a client session soon and wanted to focus on it. At ten o'clock, I called the entrepreneur I was going to work with, and after an hour and a half session, I hung up. This woman had such a wonderful mission; I couldn't wait to translate that into a website and text for her. Still, I didn't immediately sit down at my laptop. I was aware that I needed to shift my focus from head to heart in order to create what was truly intended for her. So, I walked to the front door, put on my walking shoes, and headed into the woods.

My walks in the woods helped me with my creations. I did not want to sit down and simply think everything through. Instead, I tried to be purely a channel for what needed to be expressed. Walking in nature and opening myself up to whatever came to mind proved helpful.

I had already established a set route of winding paths through the forest that eventually brought me back to the beginning of the park. In a meditative rhythm, I walked across a soft bed of dry twigs and leaves. I let go of everything inside me and focused on the surrounding nature. I threw my head back and surveyed the tree canopy. Almost immediately, I tripped over a thick tree root, and my laughter echoed through the forest. Yes, it was a reminder to stay grounded right here on earth.

At a brisk pace, I walked along the path that led me toward a slightly wider trail. Here, you could see the marks of people passing through on horses and on mountain bikes. At that moment, it was quiet, so I had no fear of being knocked over. As I walked deeper into the forest along this path, I suddenly had a strange inspiration: I was reminded of Delft blue porcelain. I had no idea where it came from, but I immediately felt a YES. This blue would look great with the red the client had in mind.

I immediately got an idea of how to build the site and integrate these colours to create an attractive whole. Now, I could hardly wait to bring this vision to life on my screen, so I quickened my pace and, after a forty-minute walk, plopped down at my computer, feeling somewhat sweaty. Now I was unstoppable; when ideas started flowing like this, they had to be realised. So, I began collecting images, building the page, mixing colors in CSS code, and experimenting with combinations that truly captured the feeling I had experienced in the woods. After an afternoon of nonstop work, I had created a website page that was structurally sound. With her mission clearly described, and her photos combining beautifully with the coloured areas, I then created a contact form with a Delft blue china pattern as a background; an eye-catcher designed to compel the reader to take immediate action.

I hesitated for a moment about that porcelain. It had nothing to do with the subject, of course. She was an executive coach, international speaker, and writer. The site needed to exude a certain level of professionalism. Still, I knew I had to use it. Creating without inhibition was my main motto. So, I changed nothing and quickly hit the submit button.

An hour later, I received a recorded message. An elated entrepreneur told me how surprised she was by my first design, yet it made perfect sense to her, especially the Delft blue china I had used as an image at the bottom of her site. Full of enthusiasm, she shared her special connection with this porcelain. She explained how she used to work with it herself, and how the fragility, yet also the strength, of this china always reminded her of her own vulnerability. It touched her immensely to see it on her own website, the place where she made herself, in all her vulnerability and strength, visible to the world.

As I overheard the message, goosebumps ran down my arms and tears welled up in my eyes. 'You see,' I whispered to myself, 'always trust what you feel!' In connection with the quantum field, I could pick up on this kind of idea and create the most amazing things, if only I didn't sit around thinking it up or analysing it to pieces. If only I dared to open up and trust. With a smile from ear to ear, I hung up. This is how we should all work with each other, with the world.

Out of boredom, I watched a talk show that evening over dinner, and the contrast could not have been greater. It focused on topics such as the bubble in the economy, people expecting a crisis, with so-called experts muddying the talk show table with more problems. Before I knew it, I was completely swept up in an energy-sucking negative current. I wasn't really aware of it at the time; I was too engulfed in my own thoughts, which were tumbling out chaotically. 'This crisis might be as bad as they say! Will my income be enough if things go quiet? Will I be able to take care of myself here in expensive Holland? Have I thought this through well enough? Should I have taken those first two weeks off?'

   Tense, as ever, I clicked through my Excel spreadsheet, summarising my income and expenses.

At that moment, there was plenty on the schedule, but whether that would still be the case the following month was a big mystery. Normally, I could work with this kind of uncertainty just fine; it always worked out. But now, as my fears were taking over, I didn't feel that confidence at all. Maybe I needed to become more visible with website building after all? I had nothing to fall back on. There were no benefits for a Dutch person just returned from abroad; I was on my own.

That feeling of loneliness, of standing on my own, was all too familiar to me. My protective mechanism knew exactly what to do: control! The fear slowly but surely seeped into my system, and before I knew it, I felt I wanted more clients. It was best for me to deviate from the 'go with the flow' approach and get a little more proactive. In other words, become more visible. I reinforced that intention by starting a meditation session. I connected with the feeling of being a successful entrepreneur, envisioning a full agenda and a bank account swelling with turnover.

As I said earlier, in the Netherlands, things were manifesting on the spot. No sooner had I set the intention than the first requests were already pouring into my mailbox. In the weeks that followed, over twenty new clients arrived via email. I didn't have to worry about money for the time being.
    When I am ON, I am ON, which means activated, energy is flowing through my body and I know that I am acting exactly according to my purpose, and that time flies when I am in the flow.'
I had to laugh at how quickly I could get things done, purely by focusing my attention and energy on them.

Was this really the right direction for my path?
    I deliberately left that question unanswered.

Chapter 25
Really Rising

One morning, amongst all the new website requests, I saw a message from somebody called Marcel. Huh? I was immediately alert. This was a man I had seen occasionally on Facebook over the past few years. I had often looked up from his posts and jokingly thought, 'I want a man like that!' I had to laugh. What was this man suddenly doing in my mailbox? As I read on, I saw he was looking for a house. He had seen my place in this community on Facebook and wondered if there was a house like that for him, too.

Because I occasionally shared something about my new home via social media, I often got requests like this. But as nice as this seemed to me, I knew Wilma had a waiting list, and nothing was available right now. Still, Marcel would absolutely fit into the group of like-minded people she wanted to shape this place with. If you don't try, you won't know, as they say. So I sent him Wilma's details and told him he could at least give it a shot.

When I ran into Wilma at the park that evening, I told her about Marcel and that I felt this man would totally fit her ideas about the park. She said that she did not expect to have space soon, but that she would certainly keep him in mind for the future.

Meanwhile, I didn't have to worry about income. My schedule filled up faster than I could have imagined. Before I knew it, I was booked for months and even had to say no to new requests.

However, when I left the last Zoom meeting a few weeks later on a Friday afternoon, I noticed how tired I was. It was really hard work now, and my art materials had been sitting in the corner, unused, since my return.

There's a saying that claims you're most effective at helping others when you're dealing with similar challenges. Indeed, I could not get enough of unravelling other people's essence, clarifying who they really were, what drove them, and making this visible. It was a process in which they also had to really stand up for what they wanted to put out into the world. Nothing could be too floaty, special, or weird for me. For me, everything that was real and authentic in another person was beautiful. I was completely turned ON with that.

"Saying what I actually do in my work or in my art…I don't know if I want to," I said to Linda one afternoon.

We had settled down on a nearby restaurant terrace. She looked at me, smiling. "You've been doing it for a long time anyway!"

"Well, it doesn't feel that way to me!" I responded scornfully. "I still feel like I'm holding back a lot sometimes. Like with my art. I can feel the potential in it, I can see what actually happens, and I sense the energy that is released in some works. But really going for it?" With a deep sigh, I picked up my coffee again.

"Then, what is it that you really do?" she asked defiantly.

"You know, the painting that you bought, the one that Elske and I created together–that was pure magic. When we finished it, and I looked at that canvas, it seemed to start moving. There was an energy in it that allowed you to make contact with multiple dimensions. That feeling of unity–that everything is one energy field, and that we can connect our energy with it–I make art that allows you to come home again."

It made me laugh nervously right away. "See, and that's what I'm not going to tell the world!"

Linda burst out laughing. "As if you could stop that! That's too funny. You always tell me to follow my heart, and now you say this about yourself!"

"It's always so much easier to feel that it's right and not so crazy sounding when I tell other people to follow their heart . Then I don't feel the fear that I feel within myself: the fear of the consequences if I really choose this."

"You know what's a good idea?" Linda sat up straight, clearly energised and ready to share her brilliant hunch with me.

Even before she spoke again, tension crept up from my stomach.

"You're always talking about those special meditations of yours. Why don't you use them to set a powerful intention to really connect with your art?"

I felt a YES and a NO at the same time.
And so, I already knew the answer.
Yes.
A heartfelt YES!'

"Yes, I want to do that. Really stand up for that part of me. Live fully, hold nothing back."

"Good, then you know what to do tonight!" With a big smile, Linda turned her face toward the sun to enjoy the warmth.

Shit, now there was no turning back. What was I going to set in motion next?

The interesting thing is, nothing stops a heartfelt intention. Because after that meditation in the evening, everything was back in alignment. And life started flowing again as before.

Thus, out of the blue, I received an email from the company that had commissioned the coin design. It was now for sale and was in great demand by collectors. They asked if I wanted to make a second design.

I didn't have to think long about that. This question made me rummage through my painting supplies for the first time since my return. I already had some ideas, and I wanted to explore them by drawing.

Right after I pulled my drawing materials out, I received a second request in the mail. PureChild magazine was planning a themed issue on autism for the next month. The founders of the magazine had been following me for years and would love to feature one of my drawings. They asked if I could tune into the power of autism and create a design.

Assignments like that were the best, ones where I could throw myself fully into a subject with inspiration. No frameworks, no expectations, just being a channel. How did autism feel? How might that translate into a geometric drawing? What energy and information would emerge?

As soon as I started drawing, the design emerged naturally. Each line inspired the next. The compass glided across the paper as if guided by an external force. I saw shapes materialising that I had never drawn before, and the image increasingly came to life. When I finished, there was a mandala-like design with one side completely geometric and the other softer and more open. I sensed that this represented the experience of someone with autism; a reality that was enormously rich. It might appear somewhat closed off to the outside world, but the knowledge and insights that people with autism hold are immensely valuable. I scanned the drawing and sent it to the magazine's editor.

    They were immediately excited and the magazine's designer turned it into a beautiful illustration that complemented the interview. A few weeks later, I received the magazine in the mail: my art was in a magazine that was going to be read by thousands of people. My heart leapt with joy.

All the momentum of the past few weeks made me feel reconnected to what really drove me: making our infinite abilities and our freedom, our essence, visible. As a result, my creativity and natural flow were also back ON. It was now up to me to move with the wave.

However, I now found myself in a dilemma. Due to my lack of confidence, I had really packed my schedule with websites to be built, while my desire and intention had set in motion a completely different path: making art, writing my book, really living my potential.

Shit, I had got myself stuck.

How was I going to manage this now?

That night, I resumed the meditation. It was good to tune into myself and my role in it all. It was time to let go of the 'how and what' again.

I was not in control.....

Chapter 26
The Survival Mode

If, on the one hand, you feel crystal clear about your purpose in this world, but on the other, you fear you cannot make a living from it, you find yourself in a painful dilemma. As long as I believed I needed to build websites to survive, leaving no time to truly follow my heart, I was trapped. This left me stuck in a vicious cycle, merely existing, always on the handbrake, caught in that confining grip that increasingly took my breath away.

Nothing is worse than feeling energy flowing, being thrust toward what is meant to be, and then finding yourself blocking this energy. Out of fear. Because I didn't know any other way. Because I didn't yet understand. And I didn't dare to take that step into the unknown. So the energy became stuck. In a short time, I gained weight, and each day I felt worse. Until finally, I woke up with such severe stomach cramps that I could no longer work at all. I thought about using willpower to overcome the fear, but my body said NO.

The abdominal pain worsened over time. For a moment, I feared I might have a serious disease, but quickly snapped myself out of that. I knew exactly what was happening. My stomach pain was a signal that something was wrong. I had completely surrendered to the narrative of fear that the media had propagated, allowing myself to be swept up in tales of crises and financial scarcity, and I let it drive me mad. This fear paralysed me, when what I truly needed to do was harness my strength.

I decided to clear my schedule completely for the time being and focus on myself. I started with fasting; my body needed nothing for a while. On the second day, I meditated to activate my pineal gland. Gradually, my body relaxed again. After the meditation, I put on a soothing playlist and lay down. Slowly, a stream of sadness welled up in my belly. In fits and starts, it all came pouring out: the feeling of having abandoned myself, of not being true to myself, and the fear of being unable to live. There was also grief from earlier times when I had no one to care for me, or wasn't allowed to fully be myself. And now, I had done this to myself.

After three hours of crying, I felt peace return. Space had opened up–a lot of space–and my stomach pain was gone. There was more air in my lungs, and slowly the crown of my head opened as well. I regained access to the field from which my paintings and writings originate. There was peace and trust there. It was real; I remembered it again. Now tears streamed down my cheeks once more, but this time they were not of sadness, but of knowing, knowing that this was important. That I had remembered it again.

That this was what I had chosen:
to create from my core,
in touch with everything.
As long as I worked in this quantum field.

Connected,
present,
real.

Chapter 27
An Old Acquaintance

By now, I had been living in Harderwijk for several months and had become completely accustomed to my house, the forest, the village, and the friendliness of the neighbourhood supermarket.

One morning, after a short walk in the woods, I ran into Wilma at the park entrance.

"Do you fancy having a cup of coffee with me this afternoon on the terrace?" she asked spontaneously.

"Oh yes, that would be nice!" I answered. Before she walked on, she said, "Hey Tess, you won't believe it, but a house has unexpectedly become available. So, I was thinking: you could move in, or you could stay in your house for a while and I could give this to Marcel. I have a strong feeling that he should come here."

"Yes, so do I," I responded without hesitation.

"You know, I'll contact him right away." Briskly, Wilma walked back into the woods. I could already see her busily tapping on her phone. I had to laugh at us: two women making decisions purely based on intuition. Well, that's how you create adventures in the moment.

That afternoon, we both plopped down on the beanbags on her terrace and enjoyed the sun.

"I've texted Marcel, and he's coming over this afternoon," she said, sipping her coffee. "How do you even know him?"

"Well, that's an interesting story," I began. "I don't actually know him personally. About six years ago, just before my bankruptcy, I got a message from him via social media, sent purely to give me encouragement. I also felt a powerful connection with him. No idea why. We've been following each other online for the past few years. I've always found him to be a very interesting man. An ex-Marine who now helps people make the impossible possible on a personal level. He's very strong physically, but also has a developed consciousness. It's a very attractive combination!" I said with a telling look that made Wilma smile.

"How cool! And exciting too. After I show him around the house this afternoon, I'll drop by with him."

"OK, great. Finally, I get to meet him in real life."

That afternoon, as I was preparing soup, Wilma knocked on the door. I quickly wiped my dirty hands on a tea towel and walked to the door. Through the little window, I saw two figures. With a firm pull, I opened the door and there I stood, face to face with Marcel for the first time.

Wow! My breath caught in my throat.

There, at my front door, stood a big, broad man with an open face, a smile, and dark blue eyes that looked at me penetratingly.

"We finally meet," he said.

"Can I give you a hug?" I asked spontaneously.

"Absolutely!" he said, already opening his arms.

That I didn't know this man at all didn't seem to matter to me. I hugged him as if I were embracing an old friend.

I felt his muscular arms wrap around me. Our energies instantly clicked, and the sense that I knew him overwhelmed me. That I had known him for a very long time. It was as if those arms had been holding me for years.

Indeed, it seemed like an eternity before we let go of each other again.

I looked at him with a smile on my face that wouldn't fade in the weeks that followed. A feeling of 'I'm so glad you're finally here' swirled through my body and I couldn't stop smiling. Fortunately, I still had the clarity of mind not to say this out loud. Instead, I asked, "So, are you coming to live here?"

"Well... I guess there's no doubt about that," he said, as he continued to look deep into my eyes.

I said nothing. Yes, it was obvious. There was really no doubt about it. This man belonged here.

"Indeed," said Wilma, who stood smiling at us. "Marcel certainly fits in here."

"How nice!" I said enthusiastically. "Well, then I guess I'll be seeing you again soon."

"Yes, I'm coming to live here in about a month. Once I'm settled, I'll come and have a cup of coffee with you," he replied.

Once again, he gave me a hug. "Thanks a lot," he whispered in my ear.

"I'm so happy for you!" I said, holding him a little more tightly.

As I walked back inside, I laughed out loud.

'Okay, I didn't see this one coming. Brilliant turn of events!'

Half an hour later, Wilma was at my door again. I was still laughing when I saw her.

"What happened there?" she asked, her eyebrows raised with curiosity.

"I know," I laughed. "I felt like I had known him for years. And yes, this sounds strange, but I had a strong feeling that he is my future partner."

I had to laugh at these thoughts that were so far ahead of the game, but it was true. The feeling was completely clear.

"Well, congratulations then," Wilma laughed, and she got back on her bike.

Chapter 28
With You, I Will Come Home

This special encounter, and the promise that hung in the air as a result, filled me with decisive energy. My physical problems also eased slightly in the weeks that followed, but I knew they would return immediately if I did not adjust my work schedule. I really had to choose for myself now. So, I made an important decision: I would quit this job. My sister, who also ran an online business, could take over my current clients, and I would not take on any new clients. This would ensure that in two months, I would be completely free. I had built up a small financial buffer of two or three months from working a lot; how I was going to make my money after that was still a big mystery.

As I was updating my calendar, a text arrived. A tingle fluttered through my stomach when I saw Marcel's name. He had arrived here a week ago and was asking if I felt like having coffee. Well, I did. By now, I had become mega-curious about this man, so I quickly messaged him back to arrange a time.

A few days later, the time had come. We had agreed to meet at seven, and with winter now setting in, it was pitch black when I walked across the park. Using the light on my cell phone, I illuminated the winding paths that led to Marcel's cottage. There, I saw his Volvo, the vintage car he liked to drive. He was already standing in the doorway when I walked into the garden. A beaming man looked at me, and, as if it were the most natural thing, we gave each other a big hug.

What a pleasure to feel this man against my body.

'Tessa!' I really had to give myself a stern talking to. 'Don't get ahead of yourself!' I reminded myself.

I let go of him and took a step back. We looked at each other in silence for a moment before he asked if I wanted tea or coffee.

"Tea, please," I replied. He disappeared into the kitchen, and I walked through his living room, curiously studying the pictures on his walls. Four beautiful daughters in his arms, action pictures from his naval days, and exuberant scenes at festivals told many stories.

When he returned to the living room with two teacups, I sat down on the couch, and he took a seat in an easy chair on the other side of the room. Enough distance to keep the evening very proper, I thought as I chuckled to myself.

We skipped the small talk almost immediately, and the conversation quickly turned to life, the potential of humanity, energy fields, creating from a non-knowing, and relationships in freedom, unconfined by the prevalent social concepts. I could hardly believe my ears; I had come across someone who thought exactly the same way about these topics. He dared to think openly, asked questions, and was consciously self aware. Before we knew it, the moon was high as we talked like old friends who had years to catch up. The energy was so powerful and palpable in the room. It built slowly but surely. Deep into the night, I gave him a hug and walked back home.

Wow, this meeting really impressed me, yet somehow, it didn't surprise me; I had felt something of great promise the first time we met.

But I also knew that I could let it all go immediately. If something was meant to happen, it would, and if not, there would be a good reason for it. By now, I really understood that I had nothing to control or analyse. Regardless of that, I was grateful for our evening together.

The conversations with Marcel also validated my decision to quit my current job and truly pursue what we had spent hours discussing that evening. I was meditating every morning again and working with the latest entrepreneurs on becoming visible. When my last session with them was over, I also felt the last vestige of resistance leave my body. It was now time for me, and I reinforced that decision with a new tattoo.

Whether it was a coincidence or not, it so happened that Wilma's daughter was a talented tattoo artist. I had met Jane a few weeks earlier, and together we had created a design. It comprised special symbols she had designed, combined with a geometric design of mine. 'I am safe,' it said in a kind of secret language.

This was an important reminder for me during these exciting times.

One Sunday morning, Jane came over to actually apply the tattoo. She used an ancient technique called hand poke. Using only a needle, she drew the tattoo on my skin, prick by prick. This method made it a long day, as the tattoo took about eight hours to complete.

She had not yet started when I heard my phone ping, indicating a message had arrived. Quickly, I looked through my messages. It was Marcel!

'I feel I should come to you. Can I come and give you a hug?' he wrote.

My mouth fell open. What did he mean by 'I need to come to you?'

I quickly messaged him back to say that a hug was always welcome, but that I would be spending hours with the tattoo artist.

'Okay, I'll come later today then, or tomorrow or the day after,' he replied, leaving me in a state of utter confusion.

In the early evening, Jane left my house. The tattoo was done. I prepared a salad and watched my favourite series.

As I rubbed my red skin gently with protective ointment just before bed, my phone pinged again.

'Are you still up?' It was Marcel.

In all honesty, I had just turned off all the lights and was heading to bed. But I didn't hesitate for a second; I had to see this man now. I was too curious.

'Yeah, sure, come over for that hug!' I wrote.

I quickly snapped all the lights back on and centred myself a bit. The tension in my stomach increased. What was going to happen here?

Less than five minutes later, I opened the door to see that delightful, smiling man again. The hug we gave each other left little to the imagination. Once on the couch with warm cups of tea, he started talking.

"Well, this is probably going to be an incoherent story because I've never experienced anything like this before. So, I'll just tell it as it is."

"Okay…" I said, nervously shifting across the couch.

"When you came over the other week and we spent that whole evening talking… I've never sat in such a powerful energy field with anyone before. The energy in the room was so intense," he said, looking at me penetratingly.

"Yes" I laughed, a little embarrassed. "I felt the same thing."

As he continued to look at me intently, he spoke seriously.

"And last night, I literally dreamed that I needed to be with you. That dream was so real, I woke up at three in the morning and just knew that you're the woman I'm going to come home to. I actually wanted to knock on your door last night." He leaned back and said with relief, "And that's why I'm here!"

What was happening here? I had never in my entire life been as surprised as I was now. My expression was a mix of 'I see water burning' and 'Was there something in this tea?' But I also felt its truth. He was telling the truth and had had the

courage to do so. Now I had to step up as well.
   "The moment you stood at my door when you came to look at your house, I just knew it, too: I knew you."
   He laughed out loud. "Okay, wow!"

This was by far the most awkward and unusual situation I had ever experienced. I had spoken to this man for one evening, and now we had just declared our love for each other. I had no idea how to handle this.

There was only one way forward: stay in the moment, don't rush into anything. Just be present.

We looked at each other.
A silence fell.
We continued to look at each other,
curious about who we really were.

Time seemed to pass slowly as I looked into the eyes of someone who I felt deep in my cells was my man. But in reality, we hardly knew each other at all. My whole body wanted only one thing: to touch him, to feel him!
   It remained silent until he asked, "What is going through your mind right now?"
   Without reservation, I said, "That I really want to give you a hug." He spread his arms, and I curled up against his muscular chest.
   Yes, this felt really good!
   With difficulty, I tried to relax as I lay against him. The energy coursed through our bodies, but it felt complicated to connect with him physically right away. I had to give myself some time to calm down and open up slowly.
   Our energies merged little by little and they pulsed palpably as we lay there silently against each other.

Then he lifted his head, and I turned my face to look at him.
   "I love you," he said.

He hadn't even finished speaking before we both burst into laughter.

"This sounds so weird, of course, but it's really what I feel!"

I totally understood what he meant, as I felt the same way. I already knew this man; we already loved each other. It was as simple as that. Slowly, his face came closer, and we kissed each other for the first time. Electricity seemed to spark off us. My body felt as if it had disappeared, transformed into pure energy. Hours passed like minutes. The first time we looked at the clock, it was five in the morning. We had literally been in another time dimension, but I had to make sure I came back to this reality for a while.

"Okay honey, I'm going home to grab three hours of sleep," he told me, and gave me another kiss in the doorway as he left.

But I could forget about those three hours of sleep. Once in pyjamas, I couldn't settle in bed. There was no way I was going to sleep. Too much was going through my head, body, and energy system. Indeed, when the alarm went off at 8:30, I hadn't slept for a single second.

But I wasn't tired. The energy of our meeting was still coursing through my body. It was abundantly clear; this might be the big game changer in my life

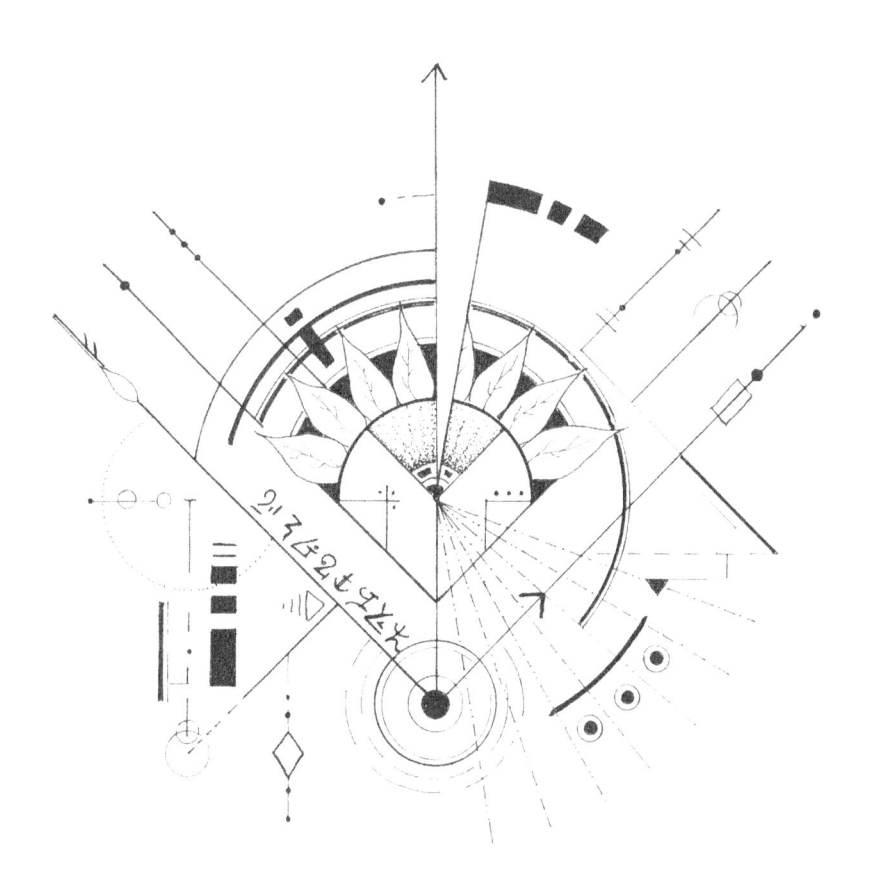

Chapter 29
Synchronicity

To all those people who loved to give me dating and love advice, saying, "Tessa, he's really not just going to come knocking on your door," I wanted to shout, "Eat your heart out!" How brilliantly had this turned out! In Spain, I had felt destined to meet a man in Holland, and that man had indeed just knocked on my door. And he was going to play a very important role. It was immediately clear to me that our relationship was going to cause fireworks. With the risk of explosion, of course.

This man was as 'ON' as I was. The energy was palpable when we saw each other. He was truly present, and with such sincerity, I felt my defences begin to fall away. I was opening myself up more, becoming softer, needing to be less hard on the outside. As a result, I felt able to connect with myself more deeply and give more space to my sensitivity.

For example, one weekday during that period, I was walking across the heath. The energy was tangible that day, as if I was walking in a kind of tiramisu of energy layers. I sat down on a bench on a hill, the sun on my face, my eyes closed. In the distance, the sound of an axe repeatedly coming down on a stump of wood echoed through the air. The blows of that axe became a kind of mantra: bam, bam, bam.

The wind through my hair,
my eyes closed,
the warm summer sun,

bam, bam, bam
the sound of the axe striking wood,
and before I knew it, I was in Spain.
Huh?
Bam, bam, bam.
And before I could react, I was back on the moors in Holland.
And then again in Spain.

It was as if I could move instantaneously, a kind of teleportation without a spaceship. Curiosity always took over when the unknown presented itself. I was careful not to over analyse this with my rational mind. No, I was going to fully absorb this new experience. I even invited it: 'Let me experience something new. Dimensions I do not yet know. Let me see them!'

So, for a moment, I felt no time, no place. I was here on the Dutch heath and on that Spanish mountain. I loved it!

The connection to Spain did not appear for nothing. That same afternoon, I saw a message from Annet on Facebook. I had met her a few times in Spain, as she was a friend of Elske's. In her message, she mentioned she was coming to the Netherlands and was looking for a place to live; a situation I had found myself in six months ago. Annet was a special lady and, in my opinion, clearly someone who belonged in our now rapidly growing community. Without hesitation, I messaged Wilma.

'Wilma, do you have anything available at the park? I know someone who I think would fit in well here, and she's looking for housing.'
   'Well, that's a coincidence. Something just became available next month. They gave notice to me today.'
   Nothing is coincidental, I thought afterward.
   'What kind of person is it?' Wilma messaged.
   And I told her what I knew about Annet. How she also

worked from the heart, that I knew her from 'making your own natural soap' workshops and the lush dreamcatchers she created. In addition, she took beautiful photographs. Before I could elaborate any further, Wilma messaged back enthusiastically.

'That Annet! I know her!'

'No way!'

'Yes, I once did a retreat in southern Spain and I met her there. She is someone with whom I feel a wonderful connection. How cool, yes, I would love to have her here as a new resident.'

Really, when everything in the field is connected, that's how it goes!

A month later, I was waiting for an exhausted Annet at the entrance of the park. Those 2,500 kilometres weren't easy; I knew all about that. So, after a firm hug, I left her alone to move into her new house. Catching up could come later.

Later that day, I walked back to my place, smiling.

"Hey, you look happy!" I looked over and saw Marcel walking toward me. I immediately gave him a big hug and a kiss.

"Hi my sweet, how did your training go? I thought you wouldn't be back until tonight," I asked as he put an arm around me.

"I finished earlier and thought it would be nice to have dinner together."

"What a delightful plan!" I said enthusiastically.

"What were you thinking just now? You were walking around the park with a big smile on your face," Marcel asked as he opened the door of my chalet.

"Oh yes, I just saw Annet and thought about how incredibly brilliant synchronicity is. For years, I dreamed of living in one place with friends. It's one of those dreams many people have, but doesn't come to much in practice. I've looked at pieces of land in Spain, imagined converting ruins into beautiful residential communities, and brainstormed for evenings with friends about communities where everyone could live freely. But no matter what I imagined, it never came to pass. And now, it has come about purely by itself. I am where I always wanted to be, with beautiful people in a communal place, in nature, each with their own home, with the intention of really connecting with each other and doing beautiful things together. I could cry with happiness."

"How wonderful, sweetheart. Let that happiness flow, I would say." Meanwhile, Marcel looked at the possibilities for our shared meal in my refrigerator, but then slammed the door shut again.

"Shall we have a nice dinner out in the village?"

"Yes, that's a much better plan." Quickly, I grabbed my bag and coat and walked out after him.

So, this life, this community, all of this was what could come into being if I stopped trying to contrive it, if I stopped trying to direct it. By connecting with my desires, with myself, and with others, everything else could manifest.

It became increasingly clear to me that this way of living had great potential. This was just the beginning!

I had a deep longing within me that had not yet fully matured: the free life I had discussed with so many friends. Living truly free, being completely yourself, no longer confined by concepts and systems. It seemed like a utopia in a society that appeared to thrive on frameworks and limitations.

Would it be possible for me to let go of my own concepts and ideas and truly create autonomy within myself? Could I really free myself and, in doing so, allow a completely new life to emerge?

A deep knowing within me said YES, but my rational mind couldn't grasp it through any conceivable means. I had no images or ideas. There was only that pure knowing: YES, a completely different world was possible.

I wanted to create it, even if it is the last thing I do on earth.

Chapter 30
Freedom

Months passed. Besides Annet, two new people had moved into the park. The community was taking shape. Marcel and I were also growing closer. It was quite exciting to be with this self-confident man, someone who also had a great desire for independence but who, at the same time, seriously wanted a relationship with me. Trust and freedom were the keys to an exciting convergence.

"What is freedom, anyway?" Annet asked out of the blue as we took our now daily walk through the woods.

"Well, it's something that has been challenging all my life!" I responded sincerely.

"How so?" she looked at me questioningly.

"I grew up in a family where speaking your mind was not permitted. 'You don't contradict your parents,' we were told. We weren't allowed to talk at dinner, and indicating that I didn't want something resulted in a corrective tap. I remember standing in front of my stepfather thinking, 'Okay, I am not allowed to say anything and you are stronger than me, fine, but what I think, you can never touch. I'll let you feel what I'm thinking.'

And so I stood in front of him with my arms crossed. I said nothing, I thought my thoughts, and sent an unmistakable energy his way. That it eventually escalated was, of course, no surprise."

"Painful and relatable," muttered Annet beside me, as we walked briskly, the memories submerging in the ground with every step.

"Yes, painful, but it also showed me that even in the crappiest situation, I was still free. Free to think, free to have my own values and standards, and free to choose my own path."

Silently, we walked on along the paths that took us deeper and deeper into the forest.

"So, freedom is within myself," Annet said, lost in thought, as she voiced one question after another while walking.

"In my own thoughts? Beliefs? What do I believe?
Dare I release myself from all those frames, boxes, and limitations?
Am I really allowed to be completely who I am?
Purely follow my intuition, joy, and heart?
Is it allowed to deviate from what everyone around me does?
Can I feel what I really want without confirmation from the outside world?
Without competing with that other person, without imposing something on that other person?"

I could see that all these questions were not currently providing her with the clarity she was looking for. They were questions that also regularly paraded through my head in a disorganised procession.

"At its core, I think it's about being purely and authentically yourself. Knowing that it is totally allowed. Just doing what you feel is true for you."

"Like that book you're working on?" she asked, challenging me. "Is it finished yet?"

A question that many in my immediate circle had been asking for months, since it had been about three years by now.

"Well, I'm pretty far along," I replied, laughing in my

defence. "I've only sent my small group of fellow readers the first half."

"Oh, and what did they think of it?"

"Well, they're enthusiastic, but also concerned."

"Concerned?" Annet looked at me with raised eyebrows.

I mentioned a message I had received from Linda the night before. She wrote: 'Tess, I think it's cool. I have a lot of respect for the open, real, and authentic way you tell your story, and I realise it's not part of freethinking, but I want to say it anyway: in my opinion you really expose yourself and your outlook on life, and I'm not sure everyone will be able to understand and feel it, let alone appreciate it. So, how do you want to deal with positive and negative reactions?'

"Oh yes, I understand her question," Annet said with a concerned look.

"Annet, this is exactly what it's about. I left out quite a bit in my first book, but I regretted that as soon as I printed the first copies. I promised myself then that I would write my second book completely freely. Shamelessly! I wouldn't withhold anything, or leave things out just to be 'safe'. No, I wanted to be real, authentic, and true.

So, yes, I know very well that there may be consequences to being so outspoken and writing passionately about a completely different view of life. That it could provoke both negative and positive reactions. But that is not important at all. The world around me doesn't have to give me permission. This is exactly what it is about."

Energised by my thoughts, I continued, "How wonderful it would be if we all dared to let go of what others think of us, so that we live purely as ourselves, expressing ourselves sincerely, and daring to share deep desires with each other. That would be wonderful, wouldn't it? Then we would really see the person next to us in their uniqueness. That person is not the same as you, nor do they think the same. But that is precisely what is so interesting. It makes it possible for us to do great things together, after all!"

Startled by my enthusiastic energy, a squirrel shot into the tree in front of us. Annet looked at me, smiling,

"You're ON!"

"This is so important, An!" I continued.
    "I won't be slowed down anymore. Remember when I made that painting with Elske? It was precisely our different painting techniques and our different approach to creating that allowed us to paint something we both could never have made on our own. So if we want to see that reflected in the world, we need everyone to be authentic again."
    "And yes, that requires courage. A lot of courage in a world full of judgments, rules, and expectations of conformity. Not with your head above the parapet, because otherwise...," I told her, making a cutting motion along my throat.

"Collectively, we seem so far removed from ourselves. How did we end up here?" sighed Annet.

Without answering, I grabbed my phone and theatrically scrolled through social media and news apps.

"Fear, which is constantly injected into our veins like a dangerous drug by media and politics. When we are anxious, An, our system automatically goes into survival mode. And to survive, we no longer feel. We keep thinking within the old frames, sticking to rules and concepts we know. That energy gives us zero room for innovation, out of the box thinking, or evolving. Collectively, getting that crap off our phones would be a good first step," I spoke firmly.

"I know," sighed Annet. "The harshness has crept into our society over decades. Can we still feel what really drives us?"
    It remained silent for a moment. I sensed her helplessness.
    "May love flow again?" I broke the silence by asking this question aloud. Annet looked at me questioningly.

"Dare we allow the love of life to flow again? Can we feel again the infinite, bubbling life energy that wants to flow through our bodies like a river? Truly living life. Present in the moment, greedily taking in all the beautiful things?"

"That sounds wonderful, but it's not what I see in the world right now," Annet said.

"You know," I wanted to end the conversation on a positive note, "stripped of all distractions, there is one place you can always go: inside. Coming home to yourself, taking a deep breath, and remembering again who you really are. That's all you have to do."

"And letting go," Annet added. "Maybe now is the time to see that no matter how much control you want to exert, you are no longer in control."

"Yes, I believe that too. That our next step in evolution may be a different one. One where we feel connected again as a whole, and that if we dare to align with that, we truly have infinite capacities as humanity. A reality in which it all comes down to trust and surrender. These are going to be interesting times," I said.

Annet and I walked the last few metres between the forest and the park entrance, and after Annet headed towards her chalet, I mused on our conversation for a while. Freedom, truly being who we are, the current system abandoned, actually living again–was I going to experience that?

Chapter 31
High On Your Own Supply

In our park, among the chalets, there was also a beautiful traditional farmhouse built in 1600. It had not been used for some time, but Sander suggested to Wilma that they convert the upstairs hayloft into a meditation room. Over several months, they transformed this beautiful space: reeds were attached to the inside of the high roof, a wood-burning stove installed, and the wooden floor sanded and varnished. It became an incredibly beautiful space.

During the years I lived in Spain, Sander had proved to be an excellent musical accompanist for breathing sessions. Together with Sandra, a friend of his who was a professional breath coach, he proposed hosting a session in this new place. All the residents of the community were invited.

I didn't really know what to expect. How could just breathing, something you did all day anyway, put you in a completely different state of being? I found it exciting and curious at the same time.

They scheduled the session for a Saturday morning. The night before, I had fallen asleep in Marcel's arms. Lately, I had been sleeping at his chalet more often, where we had intense conversations late into the night, but we also unabashedly enjoyed binge-watching series on Netflix. Our relationship had deepened, so naturally, we decided to participate in the breathing session together. That morning, after our breakfast, we walked toward the farm.

Climbing each step of the steep stairs to the hayloft, I felt the jitters building in my stomach. Arriving at the top, I saw ten mattresses were laid out in a circle in the middle of the room. Burning candles gave the place a magical look. We each sat down on a mattress and looked at each other in silence. A singing bowl in the background completed the setting. Once everyone was seated, Sandra briefly explained how we were going to breathe. We would gradually lengthen each breath, hold it, and then let it flow through again. This method would allow much more oxygen into our systems than we were used to, and as a result, we would enter another dimension; a hallucinatory experience without the use of any substances.

I was enormously curious but also felt some scepticism. How would breathing put me in such a different state? So, I decided not to hold back at all and to fully respond to the invitation. How naïve of me!

Sander had brilliantly composed the music from the surrounding speakers. As the breathing became more and more intense, the music also built up. The moment we fell into complete relaxation, when the body let go of all control and the music reached a crescendo, I shot right into the universe. I almost didn't feel my body anymore; it felt like I was travelling through galaxies. Sandra, seeing that I was miles away, came over, placed her hand on my belly, and pulled the energy from above my head back into my body at lightning speed. A grief I didn't know existed spurted up like lava from an awakened volcano. I cried and cried and cried. Grief from my early childhood flooded me; I knew this grief! This was what I used to feel: a deep loneliness, powerlessness, abandonment, invisibility, insignificance. Deep shocks running through my body allowed all this sadness to emerge from every cell. After about ten minutes, the cleansing seemed to be done, as suddenly my whole belly softened. The energy that previously always stopped halfway down my body now flowed freely from the top of my head down to my toes. A life energy I had not felt before moved through my body like a modern free dance. I suddenly felt a lot of space, and out of nowhere, a roaring laugh came up. I laughed so hard, tears streamed down my cheeks again. But now it was because I felt how beautiful life was, how much energy I actually had, and how great the joy of life was within me. A woman who was uninhibited, in complete surrender, full of the joy of life.

This is me! This is me!

I felt an incredible euphoria as the session neared its end. The music quieted down, and everyone slowly came to sit up straight again. I quickly glanced at Sander's phone and almost couldn't believe my eyes. Unbelievably, three hours had passed! I felt as though we had been lying down for thirty minutes at most.

After this session, everyone shared their experiences. Most had had a sense that they had travelled somewhere. Some to a medieval past life, others to the stars, and yet others to a world deep within the earth. Some had been emotional, and others were very peaceful.
 But the connection between us–everyone had felt it. The faces around me had clearly softened, as if they'd thrown off their protective mask and authentic persons had emerged. I felt love for everyone sitting there.

"So this is possible with your own breathing," Sander said with a smile on his face. "High on your own supply."

The group laughed. Tripping purely on breath. Who would have thought!

I carried the experience of this breathing session with me for weeks to come. Having felt so clearly my own life energy and joy, I never wanted to lose it again.

Chapter 32
The Woman In Surrender

This new experience triggered a flow of creativity in me. I wanted to paint. But I had neither the patience nor desire to work on a drop by drop painting again, which took months. No, the energy that was flowing through me and the images that came to me needed to be translated into a work of art now. As I scrolled through hundreds of photographs for inspiration, I suddenly saw a picture of a woman who seemed to be in complete surrender. The image touched me deeply. It reminded me of that wonderful experience during the breathing session.

Yes, this woman and that feeling! I wanted to capture that on canvas.

I grabbed a large canvas, 100 by 120 centimetres, and first sketched the woman onto it. She was depicted naked, throwing her head back, her breasts just barely visible, as she opened her entire being in this movement. I then grabbed deep burgundy and moss green colours and got to work. With music in my ears and the day slowly turning into night, I continued to paint, mesmerised. While most people were already hours deep in sleep, I created the first draft on canvas. Wow! That energy and my visions were captured in this painting, and you could feel it!

I was exhausted and fell into bed. Despite the fatigue, it was hard to fall asleep; the energy was still pulsing through my system.

Over the following days, I deepened the colours on the canvas, applying several coats of paint, and its intensity increased. By the end of the week, the painting was finished. Normally, it took me months to complete a dot painting, but this took just a week. And instead of an abstract geometric canvas, I had now painted a woman. It made me so happy. The energy I felt could now move much more freely. I wanted to do this more often. What a wonderfully different way of working!

I had not yet put the painting on my website when I received a message. It was from Patrick, the man who, two years earlier, had paid five thousand euros for a future painting. He absolutely loved this new work and wanted to buy it. I was ecstatic; finally, this had come full circle. This beautiful canvas validated his intention to support my art. He also emailed me to say he did not want the painting for himself, but wanted to gift it to his mother. He asked if I could deliver it to her.

And so it was that a week later, I drove with Marcel towards Twente in the northern Netherlands. The painting was on the back seat, and I had set up the navigation system to take us there. It was quite a drive across the Netherlands, but I loved road trips.

After about two hours, we drove into a small village and were soon at the entrance to the driveway of some sort of estate. An unpaved track led us through a stretch of forest before we drove into a clearing. It was beautiful there! We passed greenhouses, a vegetable garden, and barns with large glass fronts. After a few hundred metres, we parked our car in the yard of a large farmhouse.

"What a dream place," I said to no one in particular.

"Yes, this is everything we would want," Marcel also muttered. "That beautiful space with sliding doors. I could work with groups there. The place is big enough to live with several people and also receive guests. And being so surrounded by nature and silence makes it possible for everyone to come back to themselves here. It's great."

We got out of the car and our eyes widened as we walked to the front door of the farmhouse. After a moment, a cheerful woman of around 65 years opened the door.

"I've come to deliver a gift," I told her, smiling.

"Yes, Patrick told me. I have no idea what it is. Anyway, how nice, do come in."

A moment later, we were sitting with a cup of coffee and a slice of homemade cake in the upstairs room of the farmhouse. It was a warm room with a large, dark green velvet sofa and a tall window that overlooked the meadows.

This meeting was another special surprise. We were clearly sitting here with a very interesting woman. Of course, before we started our coffee, the painting had to be unveiled. She was silent when she saw the canvas. It turned out that she had recently painted the room in the exact colours of this painting, but she didn't know why. Now everything was coming together. We immediately hung the artwork, and it seemed to click right into place. Yes, this was where my lady, filled with inspiration, belonged. That was abundantly clear!

Something told me we had not ended up here by chance. However, my curiosity was answered as we shared over coffee who we were and where we came from. It turned out that this woman had been a pioneer in the field of Ayurveda and preventive medicine in the 1970s. Back then, some saw her as a witch with her herbs and natural, holistic approach. Today, she was hip and happening and ran a spa with dozens of employees.

I hung on her every word. How had she sustained herself in those days? How did she deal with criticism when her passion was so far removed from what was generally accepted? What drove her to make herself so vulnerable?

Well, vulnerable she was not. She had simply stood for

what she believed in, then and now. Deep down, she knew it was right, and that this was what she had to do. Now, all these years later, here was a spa filled to capacity with people who couldn't find help in mainstream care. What a beautiful and special person. And how inspiring. She was a shining example of not letting fear distract you, not allowing criticism to throw you off track, and always following your own heart. My painting of the woman with an open heart was in the right place. We needed more women like her.

And that woman's energy would cause quite a stir in time to come.

Chapter 33
Without Armour

The woman in surrender stirred something in me. I felt a deep longing for that kind of inspiration, but there was also significant resistance to it. This came sharply into focus within my love affair with Marcel.

In the years before, I had often wondered why it took so long for a man to come into my life again. For more than a decade, I had been single. Now that I was in a relationship again after such a long time, I understood why.

I had always been autonomous and independent, and now I was constantly running into issues within the relationship. Did I feel anxiety because I feared losing something? As a result, I wanted control, and to keep control of the connection. Could I even feel his presence? Was he really there all the time? Unconsciously, I checked on him constantly. Marcel reacted to this by withdrawing. My high sensitivity immediately picked up on his retreat, which only made me worry more. He, in turn, withdrew even further; a dynamic that drove us apart. Something was happening within me that was destructive to this relationship.

I felt my body slowly shutting down. I told myself I didn't need to be in a relationship, and that I was fine being alone with my grief, because I had been doing that all my life. At night, I would lie in my bed having anxiety attacks. I didn't understand it anymore. Then, one night when I was sleeping alone, loneliness took possession of me. A narcissistic little voice nagged in my head: 'You see, he's really not into you. He doesn't like you enough. You shouldn't be so difficult. You also feel way too much. It all becomes such a hassle.'

It became heavy, both inside me and around me.

When Marcel came by the next evening and gave me a hug, I sank into his arms for a moment with a sigh. Slowly, he lifted my head. "How do you feel?"
"Okay," I muttered.
"Okay?" He gave me a questioning look. "I don't think you were doing very well at all yesterday, and I should have been here."
I looked at him in surprise. "Indeed, I wasn't feeling very well," I admitted reluctantly.
"Shit, I knew it." I saw a dogged look on his face. "You do have to speak up, dear."
"I know, but I don't want you thinking all kinds of things or feeling limited by me."
"You're filling in for me," he interrupted, somewhat irritated.
He was right; I was thinking all kinds of things for him, trying to second guess his thoughts. I thought I could control what he thought about me, hoping to manage something. The most likely answer to that being a distrust of this man and his intentions.
"Shit, sorry," I said with tears in my eyes.
"You don't have to say sorry," he replied, wiping away the tears. "But we got into a relationship together where we would really be ourselves, no reservations, remember? So sweetie, I'm here. Open yourself."

That invitation was exactly what I wanted to hear, but my entire system tensed up. This was so difficult. It was about trust, about the fear of being abandoned, about self-confidence. Could I allow myself to be fully present? There was so much I rejected about myself. I didn't want to be someone with a traumatic past, and I didn't want to feel those emotions. I wanted to be normal. These old patterns could not be allowed to exist.

"Come here, my love."

Slowly, I lowered myself into his arms. I felt his whole body wrap around me. His hands held my shoulders firmly, and my body shook slightly. Then he gripped me even tighter. As his arms tightened around me, the intensity of the shocks in my body increased. What was happening?

The fear in my body screamed, 'Get out of here,' but I longed to surrender. I finally wanted to let go completely. The thought had barely surfaced when the grief came bubbling up like hot lava again.

Marcel remained calm. He seemed to know exactly what to do, because his powerful arms now pulled me in until they were like two vices. My back muscles tightened, pressing against him, as if I were trying to break free from a harness. A fire bubbled up within my body. I was now trying with all my might to escape my harness, and my back felt as if it was breaking under so much force.

But Marcel's counterforce was much stronger. This was exactly what I needed: someone who didn't yield to the strength I felt inside.

"Let it go, love," he whispered in my ear.

I could have screamed. I applied even more pressure, and my body shook even more violently. And then a deep sadness bubbled up. I howled like a wolf; howled, screamed and sobbed from deep within my belly.

"I'm here. I'm not going anywhere. Let go," he said.

His presence gave me confidence. It felt safe. So, I let everything go, and for the first time, I really surrendered to this intense grief.

I cried, and I cried. Deep in the core of my body, I felt myself. My essence wanted to crawl out like a wounded animal.

My body was tired: tired of holding on, of holding back, of always being in control, constantly alert in survival mode.

"I can't take any more," I cried.

"You don't have to, dear," he reassured me. This man's presence made me finally relax everything.

I don't have to anymore.
I am allowed to be.
To let go.
To finally soften.

When I looked at the clock, I saw that over two hours had passed. Our bodies were sweaty, our clothes clinging to us.

Slowly, Marcel took off my T-shirt and stripped the clothes from my body until I was naked, then covered me with a blanket. He also removed his clothes and quickly joined me under the blanket to warm us. When our bodies touched again, they seemed to merge naturally into each other. My thinking had completely switched off an hour ago; I was purely feeling. I was naked, vulnerable, soft, and open. It felt as if my back was completely open around my heart. Slowly, his hands stroked my shoulders, and goosebumps appeared with each touch. Gradually, an energy built up again, but this time it promised something different. I wrapped my legs around him and gripped him as he entered me quietly but firmly. My whole body felt him, in every cell, as he moved within me, our bodies seeming to dissolve into a field of pure energy.

Never before had a man been so close. His energy literally merged into mine. His pace quickened, and every nerve joined in this dance of love. Our climax was approaching. No more holding back, no more control, and I cried out in pleasure. His body overflowed into mine at that moment.

A deep laughter rose from my toes, a laughter that filled the air. I laughed at life, at myself, at how wonderful everything was. I laughed at happiness and love.

This was healing; this was truly releasing pain at the cellular level and reprogramming new feelings.

"A connect at the next level, my love," he whispered in my ear.

"Exactly that!" I said and reciprocated his kiss.

Completely exhausted, we fell asleep in each other's arms.

The next day, my body felt as if a train had run over it; every muscle ached, and my entire heart area, chest, and back felt open, as if someone had removed all my ribs.

'All right, so through life without armour,' I muttered to myself.

Uncomfortable? Definitely!

But my desire to be truly present in this life was greater.

Chapter 34
A New Reality

This new experience of feeling surrendered, of being increasingly present in my body, while the life energy flowed through my system, brought me new insights and ideas. I suddenly understood that the real transformation was in the shift from THINKING to BEING. It was about my presence and the energy field. Ultimately, everything was energy. Where my attention went, creation followed.

This idea was not new; so far I had applied it quite successfully to my art, to love, and to how I lived. But I was still in the comfort of my own bubble, creating within my own square metre. When I spent time on a mountain in Spain, I thought I needed to get as far away from the system as possible, otherwise I could not create my own reality. Certainly, it had helped me in the beginning to experiment without too many external stimuli. But I had come back for a reason; life was taking place at the bottom of that mountain. If I wanted to take part, I needed to step back into the world and fully live out my talent, my being, and essence.

I felt invited to take the next step: to stop thinking and make time to experiment! Until now, I had done a lot on my own, but now that I was with a man, the two of us could explore the unknown. One evening, when I suggested we try something, Marcel was immediately curious.

I placed my hand on his chest and asked him to open and close his field purely by intention.

It was as if I had put an ice cream on a hot plate; my hand

dissolved in his chest. He had opened up. But just as quickly, my hand turned cold again and became solid.

"Now you're closing up," I said to him.

"That's right," he said, surprised. "So you can really feel that?"

"Sure."

"I was just thinking about it. So that's how strong the thought is," he said.

"Yes, and so we can also create a field together, purely by intention." I saw I had piqued his curiosity.

"Okay, I invite us together into the field of unprecedented possibilities," I said, and as soon as we both closed our eyes, I felt the energy already changing.

Tingles spread like pinpricks on the top of my head. After a few minutes, it seemed like my skull was dissolving and the top of my head was completely open. Then the rest of my body followed, and we merged into the energy together. One with everything. It only lasted maybe fifteen minutes, but the experience was timeless. We both felt crystal clear: this is what we have to do. We have to be in that state of not knowing, practising, playing, feeling, experiencing!

Okay, so practising with the field, my intention, and then being fully present. Where else could I try this out?

Synchronicity is brilliant, because by 'coincidence,' the next day I could apply this experience right away in a more earthly setting. An invite came to a brainstorming session, and I went back to the office for the first time in six years! I felt some resistance to that, as if I was going back into an old system. However, that was just a thought. What if I could stay in my new energy, present, in surrender, full of life energy and, above all, without fear of anything? I felt up for it!

The intention was strong, and I stayed focused on where my attention went. Nothing got me down, and the brainstorming session was a great success. New ideas naturally arise in this energy. There, where everything is allowed, no one is restricted, fear is on leave, and the joy of creating can be lived to the fullest.

As I drove back home, an intense feeling of happiness engulfed me. What a brilliant experience this was! I could stay in my energy without having to participate in the 'old system' at all. Being purely present as myself and in my life energy was enough. I felt a new reality. It was as if I was looking into the world with fresh eyes. I was in the existing system–I was driving back home on the highway like the rest of working Holland–but it felt completely different, as if I had driven into another world. A parallel life that had always existed and into which I had stepped. To feel this, I didn't have to sit on a mountain in Spain at all! I was fully participating, I had even done office work, and I was doing it from my own new reality. Laughing heartily in my car, I arrived home feeling euphoric.

Immediately, I called Annet for a walk. We hadn't even walked up the forest path when my insights from the day started tumbling out.
    "This is what we have to do! Take our energy away from the old structures. Just that. Without resorting to any of those old ways, because then your energy is already there! No, we should direct our energy and our attention to the reality that we can create, which we don't yet know at all.
    If we all pull our energy away from the drama that currently dominates our lives, then it simply no longer exists. No lawsuit or demonstration really needs to be made for that. Not a drop of blood needs to flow for that. How genius is that! Out of mind, no more thinking or fighting."

I saw Annet was looking at me questioningly, but the energy was also contagious.

"Great to hear, Tess, but how are we going to do it, then?

We've never felt or done this before. Going into a new reality without knowing what it looks like, what it feels like, or more importantly, what the consequences are. That's mega complicated!"

"Yes, that's exactly the point. If you knew it already, then it would be an existing concept and therefore the same as the old. On the contrary, we should have no idea! We should submit ourselves completely to a new reality. Ohhh, I feel to the depths of my cells that this is exactly what needs to happen. I would like to invite everyone to experiment with it too!"

"How will you do that then?" laughed Annet. "Is the world ready for this?"

"I don't know, An, I don't know. But I do know that this is exactly what I have to share; the rest will unfold by itself."

We kept the walk short and as I walked to my cottage, I knew what I was going to do that night: write that book! Because this story had to be told.

Chapter 35
Expanding The Mind

"Sweetheart?" Marcel and I were sitting together on the couch when he looked at me questioningly. "Would you like to experience more?"
"Of course!" I replied enthusiastically.
"We could do a ceremony together sometime?"

Marcel had been guiding people through truffle ceremonies for years. The psilocybin in these truffles makes you hallucinate, and he had wonderful experiences with it. For example, he helped veterans overcome their PTSD, but also executives and investors who wanted to lose control, to feel real again. I had just watched the documentary 'How to Change Your Mind' that week. It discussed the 1960s, when these psychedelics, which are also found in LSD and MDMA, had produced incredible results.

People with cancer had got rid of death anxiety, and alcoholics suddenly were no longer addicted. It was hugely innovative. Until President Nixon decided they were illegal drugs that should be banned. All research stopped. Such a shame! Anyway, in the Netherlands, you could still use these truffles and experience their beneficial effects legally. That's why Marcel welcomed someone from abroad every week to do a session here in the Netherlands.

Until now, however, I had not felt the need to share this experience with him. My past, with a father who was an alcoholic and manic depressive, and who had gone into psychosis after certain medications, had left a clear imprint on me: don't do drugs.

In addition, I was quite sensitive to all kinds of stimulants, whether it was sugar, coffee, or alcohol. Small amounts caused major reactions in my body. I knew I had to be careful with this.

"I have studiously avoided drugs all my life," I explained.

"It's not a drug, my sweet. The truffle is not a magic mushroom, and it's not addictive. In fact, it's at the very bottom of the list of stimulants, a list, by the way, where alcohol is at the top," he said, looking at me meaningfully.

"It's a great way to really experience other dimensions. But you have to do what feels right, of course," he continued.

Despite the reluctance in my mind, I had long since sensed the answer. Yes, I was ready for the next step, because I was too curious about what I did not yet know. It was time for one of those transformative truffle sessions.

"Fine, I'll do it!" I told him.

Marcel didn't let me repeat that and immediately went to order our truffles. The next weekend, we would have a ceremony together.

In the days before the ceremony, I drank no alcohol, no coffee, and ate no processed foods. This way, my body could enter the session as clean and light as possible, which would enhance the effects of the truffles.

On Saturday evening, the time had come. Marcel lit dozens of candles in the living room, and a quiet fire was crackling in the fireplace. There was a light scent of incense, and he had placed cushions on the floor. Two meditation cushions facing each other marked the spot where we would begin this experience together.

I had put on warm sweatpants and a thick vest. Quietly, I sat down on one of the meditation cushions and folded my legs over each other. On a small table between us were several bowls containing chocolate, nuts, and chips. 'That's a good start,' I thought. A candle graced the centre. Next to it were a wooden board, a knife, and the truffle.

The energy was already rising, as were my nerves. Was I sure about this? Was I really going to ingest something that could cause me to completely lose my way? But once again, my curiosity overcame my fear.

Before cutting the truffle, Marcel asked me to speak my intention. It came out smoothly: "I want to feel who I really am and experience self-love." Boom! My intention was clear.

Marcel handed me the tray of truffles.
   "Now, with that intention in mind, you are going to cut your own truffle into very small pieces, as small as possible. And while you are cutting, just ask the truffle to show you exactly what you need to see."
   I grabbed one truffle from the tray. They looked nothing like the expensive variety I loved to grate over my pasta. These were more like wizened walnuts with mold on them. And I was supposed to eat them. Ugh!
   Together, we silently cut our truffle into small pieces. In the background, the kettle was already bubbling. After cutting everything up, Marcel seized two large glasses, placed the truffle pieces in them, and poured boiling water over them.

A moment later, we were both sitting with a glass of tea in our hands. Carefully, I took sips of the substance that was about to do all sorts of things to me. It tasted bitter and earthy, prompting me to pull a disgusted face. Quickly, I grabbed a piece of chocolate to get rid of the taste. After finishing the tea, I looked at Marcel expectantly. Was it going to happen now?

He saw the question on my face.

"It will take a while, dear. Just sit back and relax on the couch. Observe what's happening in your body; you'll notice it naturally."

I sat back quietly. After about five minutes, I said impatiently, "I don't think it's working." Marcel smiled but said nothing.

After about ten minutes, my eyelids grew heavier. I just kind of lay down on the couch and closed my eyes. Slowly, something began stirring within my body. A tingling in my legs, chest, and head made me feel as if I was going to pass out. For a moment, I felt anxious–was I going to be all right? But I quickly let that thought go. I took a few deep breaths and allowed the tingling to intensify until it felt more like waves of energy moving through my body.

I slipped away, similar to the sensation you get when you're about to fall asleep, only this time, I didn't fall asleep. Instead, I found myself in a vortex of colours. Everything around me moved, and I saw the most amazing colours and images. They flowed together and then separated again to form new images, as if I were walking through an Escher painting.

I burst into laughter. I opened my eyes and looked at Marcel. Coloured lines now seemed to dance around his face.

"Do you see this too?" I exclaimed. "Do you see this too? It's amazing!"

Marcel laughed too. "No dear, I don't see what you see, but welcome to this new world."

Slowly, I felt myself sinking again, but now I surrendered much more easily. I was no longer afraid at all. This world seemed familiar to me, though I had no idea why. It felt familiar. This is what I wanted more of. I was as happy as a child, shifting from one reality to another. It gave me so many insights into how multiple dimensions worked, how colourful everything could be, how infinitely beautiful we could make reality.

"How hard we all work in life!" I exclaimed, laughing. "There's no need for that at all; everything is already here!"

I tried to look at Marcel again, but even with my eyes open, everything was distorted. I saw coloured geometric codes running around his head. When I looked through my eyelashes, everything changed from purple to blue. Cosmic portals opened up, through which all sorts of things flowed. Suddenly, a landscape of the most amazing colours appeared: I saw mountains, a waterfall, and a river flowing through the landscape.

I tried to touch it with my fingers, but in reality, I was lying on the couch, my fingers poking at air.
"How brilliant this is!" I cried out. "This is so beautiful."
Tears now ran down my cheeks–not from sadness, but from intense happiness over all the beauty I was seeing.
"So this is how colourful it can be," I said to no one in particular, and I heard Marcel burst into laughter again in the distance.
"What a boring, shitty world we have made of it," I continued. "So this is what we can also do."
And in that moment, I experienced exactly what I had just failed to reach with meditation all those years. That sense of unprecedented possibility was now a reality. I could feel it, touch it, see it, and play with it. The possibilities were indeed unlimited, and they were there for the taking in this reality.

"Why did we make such a grey mess of it?" I was talking, but five seconds later I didn't know if I had said it out loud or if I was hallucinating.
"Did I just say that out loud?" I asked Marcel for the umpteenth time, who then confirmed aloud that I did indeed

just say that out loud. Whereupon I immediately disappeared again into a new world and wondered again whether I had just said it out loud.

I found this thin divide between dimensions truly amazing. This was what I had always tapped into while painting, coaching, or meditating, but it had never been so palpable, so real! So, this was possible. I also felt that this was the field of dying and experienced peace like never before.

The fear of death was completely gone, and with that, a lot of other fears dissolved. How wonderful this was! This space was free of concepts, free of everything. It was truly free. My tears of joy continued to flow.

Again, I entered a wildly churning river of colours, shapes, and images. This was who I was, and I suddenly understood where my art came from. It was what I had always felt, what I was already connected to! This revelation filled me with happiness. What I was painting was right. It was right! And again, I disappeared into a sea of the most fantastic figures and images. As I travelled through this ultimate otherworld, I tried to remember everything I saw, attempting to make mental pictures of these wonderful images. But it didn't work at all. There was nothing here to grasp, or get a grip of. Surrendering was the only thing needed to create even more, and that's what I did.

Now and then, I came back to reality a little, and then I saw Marcel in a contorted position, doing a lion's roar or moving busily with his hands. I looked at him and saw his face switch from ordinary to devilish, to someone from ancient times, from human to wolf. With each roar, his face got bigger, as if he was blowing himself up like a balloon.

Normally, that would have caused me considerable anxiety, but I felt no fear at all. I was in a fear-free state of being, an experience I had never had in my entire life. My usual alert state, my feeling unsafe, my insecurities, they were all gone.

How wonderful this was! My pure essence was revealing itself more clearly to me by the minute.

Suddenly, I remembered the intention of self-love I had set before the session started. Oh yes, I wanted to feel that. How did self-love feel here? I hadn't even fully formed the question in my mind when I got an instant answer. That question was completely irrelevant here, nonsensical really. Now, I laughed at my question. Of course, I loved myself. I was wonderful; a wonderful woman. Being concerned with what others thought of me was completely uninteresting in this reality, and it made me laugh so hard. I felt only myself, in full glory. And what a beautiful woman this was! You bet I loved her.

Then the music changed to a tribal-like beat. My body wanted to move with it, and as Marcel tried to rally all the male lions on his journey, I felt my femininity increase at a chilling speed. My body moved like a snake. I squirmed across the couch; the energy surging through my body.
   "I'm a ribbon, I'm a ribbon!" I cried.

In this reality, so much more was palpable. The temperature kept increasing. I felt as if I was bursting out of my body, like lava out of a volcano.
   "I'm getting hot. Hot!" I declared, as I took off my vest and my socks. Sweat covered my back. "I'm hot," I said to Marcel, who didn't seem to be bothered by anything.

"My body is too tight for this energy," I explained.
   I tried to stretch my body, curving my back in a way that many a dancer could learn from. I felt my body from head to toe: the feminine energy, the fire, the passion. Suddenly, I realized how much power I possessed. I had always known this intensity, but had never allowed it. Now, I did.

This was ultimate freedom. I felt how strong I was. Here was the beauty, here I felt the love for myself. My body seemed to become infinitely large. And then, out of nowhere, with a rush from above my head, the entire universe came rushing through my body like a freight train. Truly, the entire universe–galaxies, planets, black holes, everything–raced through my system.

"I give birth to the universe!!!" I screamed.

Then the earthly shifted to more space, and before I knew it, I saw myself as the captain of my own spaceship. I didn't doubt for a moment; this was where I had come from. A deep purple light surrounded me. I saw the technology in which I lived, the peace and serenity. In the universe, I saw all the blueprints. They looked like building plans or intergalactic attack strategies, perhaps. Was it war? Was I on the side of light? Was I some kind of architect?

With a flash, I was back on Earth and saw myself in a robe, sitting on a horse. Next to me, Marcel rode his own steed. Together, we went to war. We came to bring the light.

After about five hours, the effect of the truffle waned, until eventually we were back in our daily reality. But I knew I would carry this experience with me forever. I had now seen it, felt it, and experienced it. No one could take this away from me. This was what a colourful life and world could look like. By now, it was dark, and after a small snack, we both went to bed, exhausted.

Chapter 36
Euphoria

In the ceremony, I lucidly felt who I was, what I was capable of, and what we as humanity are capable of. It was magical and its beauty unparalleled. I wanted to capture every image on canvas, with colours that made this world seem dull, and shapes beyond any imagination. During it, I had felt powerful, fearless, connected, and confident and had seen my origin, my essence, as well as being able to contemplate my role in this world.

But the next morning, as I slowly returned to earth, I felt gravity like a sledgehammer smashing my euphoria into thousands of pieces.

I had felt my potential. This was all I wanted to come and do. But what a failure I was in this life! Delivering less than five percent of what I had felt; I was barely living up to who I potentially was. I was failing myself and the world around me.

Grief erupted like a primal cry, and I cried like a whale that had lost its young. The sound pierced me to my marrow. I had lived in a straitjacket all my life, feeling constricted from childhood. None of this should have been my reality. I had kept myself small, restrained, and had played it safe. And for what?

When the sadness had passed, strength returned. I was not going back to the way things were. Having experienced what was possible, there was no going back. This new information was now etched into my cells. All I had to do was embrace this field of energy. To acknowledge my own powerful presence. Literally, that. The field I felt was so strong; I even felt as if my neighbours within a five-kilometre radius were now all awake in their beds.

I knew what I had to do.

I asked Marcel to join me in making this field even more powerful and immediately felt our energy merge into a great, powerful, pulsing current.

"With this, we can turn on the whole world!" I shouted out euphorically. I was so grateful to have encountered a partner who understood what I was doing and feeling, who had the same desires and curiosity, and dared to act on them.

After this mind-blowing experience, nothing was what it used to be. What did I find most brilliant? The ability to truly reprogram. All the efforts I put into meditating for years, I achieved in just a few hours here. The neuroscientists had also defined this: to really change anything, to enable new perspectives, you need to rid yourself of your old patterns and beliefs. Now, I possessed an unprecedented ability to feel what I wanted, but because a fear of living life still lingered in the background of my subconscious, that intention was constantly negative messages.

How was I supposed to let my body experience that it had nothing to fear? How could I feel it when I didn't know the experience? But, thanks to this truffle trip, I could now. In it, I had literally experienced what it was like to be without fear. After that ceremony, the restlessness I felt and the panic attacks that occasionally came along had all but disappeared. What I had struggled with for so many years was now resolved by one magical journey.

I wished this for everyone. This experience could cause the

world, as a collective, to find itself again. It would clearly feel its potential, and people would dare to connect with each other again.

"I choose this, living my full potential, even if it has consequences," I said with tears in my eyes as I looked at Marcel.

"I know, dear. You have to choose this, no matter what."

Chapter 37
Thank You For Your YES

The release of fear seemed to come in stages. Just when I thought I had really dealt with everything and it was flowing again, I'd become aware of a new layer of protection. And usually, a situation emerged where it was possible to heal it.

As nice as 'healing' sounds, it wasn't as Instagram-pretty as it might sound. Mostly, it came unexpectedly. Often, I'd have been feeling for a few days that I wasn't quite comfortable in my own skin, with sadness struggling to the surface. And usually, I successfully pushed it away for a few more days with distractions like eating, Netflix, and sleeping. But that couldn't last forever. There was no escape; something had to be faced again.

Just like that one morning in May when I cried and felt my chest tighten again. I couldn't breathe. Was this an old-fashioned panic attack? Marcel came to sit behind me again and remained calmly present as an anchor. This allowed these emotions to flow freely. The fear was allowed to be there.

   When this fear had left my body, I lay relaxed again in my man's arms.

My man!
Suddenly, it dawned on me.
This is him.
This is my man!

I knew Marcel was my partner, but I was now suddenly aware that I had not yet truly acknowledged him as my man.

I had to let him take his place.

Until now, I had never felt the confidence to do that with anyone. My protection was about being independent, being able to do everything on my own. But now, I felt how the space next to me was truly there.

I sat up straight. Marcel looked at me questioningly.

"Sweet, can you sit up for a moment too?" I asked him.

He pushed himself up and looked deep into my eyes.

I swallowed some tension. Was I really going to say this?

"I want to ask you if you would take the seat next to me, my man's seat?"

It was so much more than a proposal. The question came from deep within my being. He felt it too, and I could see that the question touched him.

"Yes, dear, I very much want to take that place."

Tears welled up in my eyes. This was so pure. For the first time, I gave a man his place beside me.

We said little, but the energy between us built, and I felt the flow. The power of the coming together of the feminine and masculine was palpable.

It was a sexual energy, a creative flow. This time, however, we didn't allow ourselves to be taken into a lovemaking session; instead, we let the energy build and build. The energy became so powerful that it seemed we might explode apart.

For the first time, I felt the potency of the masculine and feminine coming together, a place where we were truly free.

Free from any limiting thought. This was not about relationships. This was about the potential of us as humanity. We needed to reunite the healthy feminine with the healthy masculine.

"We can change the world with this energy!" I almost

shouted. "We can explode the universe. Anything is possible!"

"Yes, yes!" Marcel stood up and looked at me, smiling. "But shall we have lunch first?"

That afternoon, we drove north. Marcel had a surprise, and I got into the car mega-curious.

After an hour's drive, we had left the highway and entered the polder. This is an area of low-lying land surrounded by Holland's famous dikes. At walking pace, we drove along a dirt road lined with willow trees that seemed to welcome us with a deep bow. After a few minutes, Marcel parked the car in the grass, and we walked between the meadows to a small chapel.

"Where have you brought me?" I asked, smiling.

"We have tickets to Camie Bonger's Transformation Theatre," he said mysteriously.

That didn't tell me anything at all. But it sounded good.

Together with other visitors, we arrived at the building and went inside. We hung up our coats and then entered the small hall together. The sun shone beautifully through the stained glass windows. Around thirty people were seated in a circle of chairs, ready for the performance.

After about ten minutes, everyone was inside, and silence was requested. From behind two white curtains, a colourful young woman in her late twenties, full of energy, entered the floor. She wore a dark green dress with gold stars, styled like those from the 1950s.

She immediately began her recitation. Rhythmically, she told a story about 'No-Man's-Land Children', the children who had never felt at home anywhere, who were now searching, who recognised each other when they looked into each other's eyes. The No-man's-land children were free, because they were not bound, and they came to bring something to the world.

Everyone in the circle was touched. Tears flowed. This woman's words struck a chord deeper than what was visible. A strong connection was palpable.

Finally, she concluded her talk and told us that besides her regular theatre performances, she also organised these gatherings. She felt that we like-minded people needed each other. She knew deep down that it was time to step up to the plate with her sensitivity and talent.

"We women," she said, as she stepped onto a box, "have learned in the past, for many generations back, that sticking our heads out literally meant losing our heads. So, since then, we have held back, made ourselves invisible and submissive. But those days are over. Our heads won't come off anymore. We women have to stand up, start taking our place again, mount the crate, and make ourselves heard."

A silence fell.

"You're not going to leave me standing here alone, are you?" she asked, looking at me with her piercing eyes. I felt as if she was directly talking to me. And her question hit me deep in my heart.

"It's time that we really come to do what's meant to be. And we need each other. Even if it's hard, even if it has consequences."

I felt her invitation deep in my cells. Seeing this woman standing here in all her vulnerability and strength, I admired her. And indeed, I felt I could not leave her standing there alone now. Yes, I also had to fully claim my role. Her call had set my heart on fire.

Then, she told the group about the soul poem. Anyone who wanted to could ask her a question. She would then sit down in front of that person, make contact in silence, and from that moment on, let the words flow out intuitively–the soul of the other person, speaking through her. This was improvisation at the next level.

"Who has a question?" She looked around the room.

A woman in her forties raised her hand and shared her question. Camie sat down in front of her. I felt the energy change. Poetry flowed out of her mouth like honey, the words landing one by one, and they felt so true! I felt that Camie did not think this up, but literally let it come through her. Like I painted, she was creating a poem in the moment. The connection between the two women was truly magical, and the message was well received.

"Thank you for your yes," she said to the woman sitting across from her.
   Then she looked around the circle and repeated "Thank you for your yes," again.
   At that last word, her gaze stayed with me and she looked deeply into my eyes. I recognised this woman, and I knew exactly what she was trying to tell me.
   "Thank you for your YES," she said again, without breaking her gaze from mine. Tears sprang to my eyes.

After she had answered several more questions, she looked around the circle and walked decisively toward us.
   "I've been feeling all evening that I want to do a poem for you, may I?"
   Marcel and I looked at each other in surprise.
   "Yes, of course you can."
   "Do you have a question?"
   "No, just let flow what really needs to be said," Marcel replied.

And before I knew it, the energy changed again. Camie made contact with us, and after a few seconds she became absorbed in the words that came out of her mouth like a wild river, while looking at Marcel:

I'm feeling emotional

*I'm feeling emotional
because it's a lot
because you
you changed the plot
you came here and stood up
and for that I want to thank you
there aren't many who see this clear
and choose to rise up for the new woman
but you did the work to stand here
and so I really must say
Thank you
I appreciate that you're here today
Because you are the King we have been waiting for
a soft strength that we adore
a superpower so supreme,
I mean
in this circle we all feel it
you are here to heal it
we see it
and we all agree
your eyes shine with a different light
they clearly see
so much, so bright
and sometimes you really don't know
where all those feelings are supposed to go
Because 'hello, I am a man! That's one of those things that I just can't.'
And now finally you realize that actually, you can
and that you have permission
to feel
and be seen
and we see you
we need you
because you came and stood right here beside us, equally
in sympathy
Not with a 'woman I'm better than you' attitude
Or with an 'I'm sorry I exist', that brings you out of balance*

You stand here in equivalence
your friendliness makes a difference
Now here you are the two of you,
equally brilliant,
equivalently kind
and of course sometimes, when it gets too much
you just go out of your mind
But together you say yes for the whole
the whole and complete collective goal
yes for us all
not just for anyone
Not for you alone,
because with many, we are one
What you are doing is for all of us,
we're still searching for examples
of how to build equal relationships,
with unions as temples
So thank you both for your yes,
for continuing to love
and learn
and integrate, and discern
and every time, again and again
and over and over, and again

And without pause, Camie turned to me to continue:

Of course, if you haven't had that solid ground before
you will think 'euhhhh, that doesn't exist'
Just let it all out
get real loud
make the choice and persist
If you have nothing to lose
at any moment you can choose
for love, every time again
Thank you for standing up
and being willing to take this on
you are wonderful, mighty, super powerful and oh yes, you can

All of this came together for greater dreams to come
dreams of a new world coming true
If this goes together
and flows as well,
we will not know what to do
that's going to be a creative expression, you really have no clue
A collision of planets
this is sacred
So please,
make it safe
and even safer
Speak it out loud
give it back to love, every time around

I am here, always near
I am there, speaking in glory of another story
but I will always be there for you
All of the above,
in pain and in love

After the last word, the room exploded with energy, and the group clapped and cheered. This woman, who had never seen or spoken to us before, delivered a message in the moment that rang true. It really reflected what we had experienced together that morning. We were empowered by what we had felt.

Magic did not cover it. This is how it works. How each one of us comes to do what they have to do and how we then have important messages for each other and play our part in the whole.

She walked back to the edge of the circle and began the closing of the evening. When the session ended and everyone was getting ready to leave, I walked toward Camie.

"Woman, you don't want to know how spot on this was!"

She smiled shyly.

"We had an experience this morning where we literally discussed how powerful the energy was in our being together. How we could explode planets, the universe."

"No way!" exclaimed Camie.

"Yes, really incredible, so attuned. You inspired me tremendously. You just do it, you do what you have to do. Totally. Completely. Deep bow."

"Thank you," Camie said modestly.

"I still find it exciting, too," she continued. "But meetings like this help tremendously in this adventure. We really need to do this together."

I felt tonight's message was crystal clear. We had our place to take, to come and do what we really had to do, regardless of the consequences. Whether it was going to make us famous, or destroy us completely, it wasn't about that. It was about feeling what was needed right now.

"Yes, sacrifice," Marcel said, as we discussed this further in the car.

"I know that feeling all too well from my Marine past. Truly wanting to give your life for the greater good. How can we as humanity evolve, really take ourselves to the next level if everyone wants to stay in comfort? We will simply have to take risks, otherwise, nothing will change."

As Marcel drove us back into civilization via the highway, my thoughts wandered for a moment.

Deep down, I knew exactly what it was about, what I had to say. Staying faithful to what I knew to be true was important. How the world dealt with it or how people would react to it was not important.

I no longer wanted to be distracted by the drama in the world, the fears, and the limiting beliefs we projected onto each other.

"The more you start doing what is truly authentic, what is truly right in your life, the more resistance you will generate, both in yourself and in the outside world," Marcel said after we had sat in silence in the car for a while.

"Sweetheart, it's about staying put. Staying with yourself. Feeling. Getting out of that head. Into the body. Staying with your own truth. If that means being mistaken for crazy, you know you're on the right path." He sounded pretty driven by the idea.

"'First they ignore you, then they laugh at you, then they fight you, and then you win.' Wasn't that a quote from Gandhi?" I laughed.

Marcel laughed too: "And none of these phases has anything to do with you. Give what you have to give. Stay true to the truth, no matter how unpopular. It is of service to the greater good and so it is not ultimately about you."

Easier said than done, I thought silently.

One day, I saw with complete clarity what I had to do: I came to empower our souls with my paintings, writing, and my being, reminding us of the great powers we carry within us. I felt I had to bring people together as well. I was there to activate the realisation in all of us that together we can create a new world.

On other days I wondered if I was going crazy with delusions of grandeur. On days like that, anxiety got the upper hand, and I lay back with a cramped back or chest, crying out in my discomfort.

Yet, things also went more and more smoothly; it was only fears and old patterns that were still holding me back. The more I released, observed, and healed my emotions, the easier everything flowed.

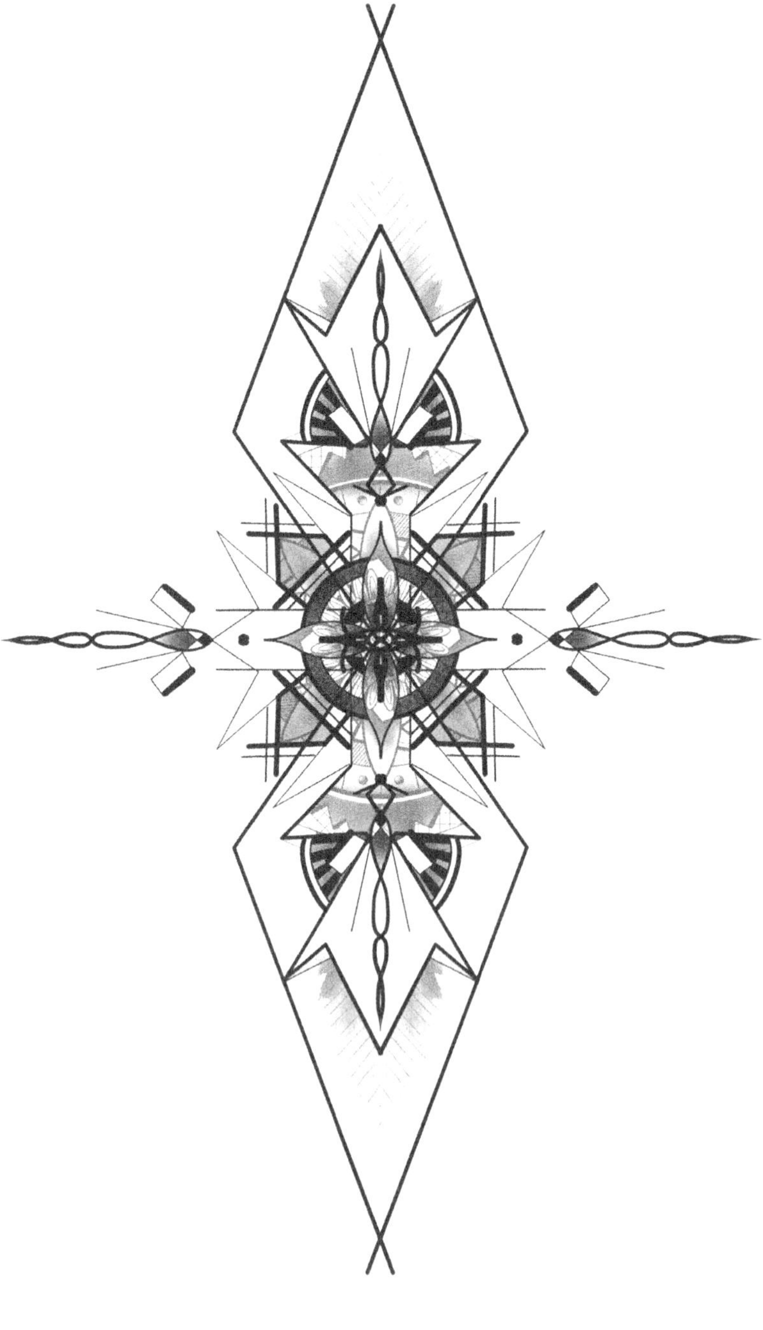

Chapter 38
The Mother's Wound

That Saturday in the chapel with Camie had stayed with me. Feminine power and the ability to create could re-enter the world. The realisation that we all had to stand up became increasingly clear to me. We could not let someone else do the work alone.

I felt strongly that I wanted the woman within me to fully emerge. Could I fully embrace life? Could I dare to surrender to everything and then truly create without limits?

It all sounded wonderful, of course, but it certainly didn't feel like an easy feat. When I looked at the world, I mostly saw women who stood their ground, women who protected themselves, women who sought to make themselves equal to men by participating as assertively as possible.

Equality in the age of emancipation was, of course, a fine aspiration. But it had resulted in a type of equality where both men and women governed the world with as much male energy as possible, suppressing the feminine aspects on both sides.

Equality should be about allowing women to fully embrace their femininity and men their masculinity, recognising and treating each other as equals despite our differences.

We must first acknowledge the value of both aspects. The stable energy of men provides a foundation that allows the chaotic, creative energy of women to flow freely. This elusive female energy is crucial because it has the power to truly create. Together, these energies are capable of achieving unprecedented possibilities.

I felt that my feminine essence was about softening. This softening could lead us away from rigidity, away from overthinking, away from the cerebral. For me, it involved trust, surrender, intuition, slowing down, and vulnerability. As a woman, I took inner leadership of this soft power and broke free from the shackles of my trauma.

But, something crucial needed to be addressed…

During a weekend trip, everything came together. Marcel had rented a cottage from friends who had bought a farm in Friesland a few years ago and converted one barn into an Airbnb cottage. We arrived in Friesland too early and decided to keep driving around. We travelled down one dirt road after another, admiring all the beautiful farmhouses. Soon, we were fantasising about owning our place and all the wonderful things we could do there. As we drove around, I kept noticing a familiar place name on the signs: Ippeldym. At first, I ignored it, but there was no escaping it. At every intersection, there it was again. It was the village where I had spent my entire childhood, an idyllic place in Friesland, filled with memories of insecurity, aggression, and loneliness. The farm where I had grown up now appeared in my mind like a dark memory.

Every time the place name appeared, I thought maybe I should go look at that farm. But as quickly as that thought came, I pushed it away. No way! I was afraid that seeing the farm again would conjure up all kinds of traumas.

But every time we passed another road sign, and I saw 'Ippeldym,' I felt compelled to visit.
   It took about three quarters of an hour before I said to

Marcel, "Dear, there's something that keeps coming to mind."

"What is it?" He looked at me questioningly as he pulled up to another intersection.

"Well, see that sign over there? With the place name Ippeldym?"

"Yes."

"That's where I spent my childhood. The farm where I grew up is there. It was a dark period. And yet, I feel the urge to have a look. What do you think?" I asked the question, hoping he would say it was a bad idea. Alas, he didn't.

"Dear, if you feel that strongly, there's only one thing to do, you know that too."

And he steered the car toward the village I hadn't been to in over 35 years.

A knot in my stomach tightened more and more. The farm represented so much fear, oppression, and insecurity. In my mind, it was an intensely dark place, a dilapidated farmhouse overgrown with weeds, harbouring deeply buried memories.

About ten minutes later, we drove into the village. I recognised everything as if it were yesterday and knew exactly how to get to my old home. We went through the village, across the bridge, down a road to the right, and finally into the cul-de-sac that ended at one place only. I was amazed. All the houses along this road had been dilapidated at one time, but by now they had been bought up and transformed into beautiful homes. A lot had changed in 35 years.

The dirt road of the past was now paved with concrete slabs, making the farmhouse much easier to reach. When we arrived at the end of the road, I saw the place looming before me.

The farmhouse was hidden in a small forest. I took a deep breath. When I looked up to observe the house, my breath caught in my throat. Perplexed, I stared at the place I had feared so much.

The horror, the darkness, the shadows of the past had given way to something beautiful.

"Wow, it's become a dream place," I stammered.

"Honey, look at it, it's beautiful!" I said to Marcel as I got out and walked around the car.

The new owners had installed a beautiful glass front on the barn and painted the woodwork a deep, dark blue. The garden was meticulously maintained, and the trees glowed with beautiful fall colours. It was truly the most beautiful place I had ever seen.

Marcel also stepped out of the car and looked at me.

"What touches you so much now, dear?"

"That the place has transformed so much. As if the earth has absorbed all the dark energy. Light and love have conquered here. It gives hope that even the darkest places can be transformed. That even here, there is fertile ground and beauty again."

As I stood there, I asked the earth to take in my painful past and darkness, to heal it, to cleanse it. In my mind, I let everything I wanted to get rid of flow into the earth. A few minutes later, I got into the car and asked Marcel to leave. Revisiting had been good.

As we drove toward our cottage, I let this magical experience sink in for a moment.

"How nice that you listened to your hunch," Marcel said.

"Yes, it's really incredible. It feels so healing to have seen it."

"Dear, we could reinforce this positive experience by doing a truffle ceremony together tonight. Then you can put this behind you once and for all," Marcel suggested.

"Oh, that seems like an excellent idea. I would like to take this beautiful transformation on a journey."

Once installed in the cottage, we began the ceremony that evening. We laid out trays of chocolate and chips, and with a beautiful intention of transformation, I cut my truffle into tiny pieces.

Moments later, Marcel poured the hot water into the mugs, and before I knew it, I had drunk the last drop.

Images soon emerged that were familiar to me. The most beautiful colours and fantastic shapes blended together to create extraordinary geometric landscapes. I was home again, in this reality where everything was possible, free from any protective mechanism. I felt again like that strong woman, powerful and soft, full of talent, love, and light. My pure essence was revealing itself to me again, and I was deeply happy.

After an hour, the energy shifted. Marcel entered a dark patch; he roared like a lion and his whole being transformed into that of a werewolf. Initially, I remained present, drawing from my feminine strength. I placed my hands on his back, feeling the animalistic power surging. Like an Amazon, I endured this ordeal.
    But then, out of nowhere, I came back to reality. I opened my eyes and felt shocked. Shocked at us there in that cottage, shocked at Marcel's roaring. What if someone came in now? What would they think? They might call the police. We could be arrested. It felt unsafe. Unsafe!

Fear entered my system like a thick mudslide. Gone was the feminine power, gone the Amazon. I felt myself being dragged along, into the depths, toward the horror I knew so well from the past. I was a child again.

This was the fear from my childhood. It was dangerous,

unsafe, and there was no way out. I felt trapped! Panic overwhelmed me. Darkness squeezed my throat. I experienced how my pure essence, what I was when I came into this world–my life energy, my joy, and my talent to create–had been destroyed by this aggressive, all-consuming masculine energy. It had destroyed my beautiful being.

Deep, deep sadness overwhelmed me, alongside the sense of the total destruction of who I really was. And there, in that darkness, I saw how this experience had made me decide not to be truly present anymore. How truly living was no longer an option for me. It was too unsafe. I closed myself off, left where I came from, and left behind a lifeless body. This was how I had struggled through life for years: surviving, keeping myself safe through control, and being present as little as possible.

My breathing slowed to a slightly calmer pace, and the big breaths of grief transformed into a soft cry. And in that moment, I saw my children. My children!

   I had never had children, but now I saw them. I knew immediately that they were mine. These powerful souls that I had not brought into the world. I bowed my head and apologised. 'Sorry!'

'Sorry for not letting you come.
I didn't want to do this to your pure souls.
I didn't want to do to you what I went through,' I told them silently.

With this deep sadness, I took a seat on the couch. Marcel, who by now had stopped roaring, came to lie with his head on my chest. Suddenly, the energy changed again, and I became his mother. He had just been born, and I was looking at my son.

   I felt how this mother had no idea how to protect such a pure soul in this harsh world. She therefore decided that living fully was too dangerous. He had to go into hiding, make himself small, because otherwise the danger from the outside world was too great. What sadness. In the role of mother, I mumbled, "Sorry, dear Marcel. Sorry that I couldn't protect you. That it was too much for me."

The energy shifted again, and a new dimension opened up. A tear ran down my cheek and I was Mary. I had Jesus in my arms and felt the same sorrow; the sorrow of all mothers who could not protect the purity of their children. And the vicious cycle became clear. The men had not been allowed to be themselves. They had to toughen up, man up. The maternal wound was deep. The men, not being seen as their true selves by their mothers, became closed off to the purity of women. That softness had become dangerous for them and it had taken everything from them. The woman was so unsafe that she became the enemy. And therefore, she in turn was made small, curbed, and destroyed by the masculine. Thus, both traumas sustained each other. Both men and women were victims. Both were wounded.

After about five hours, the effects of the truffle tea wore off, and we emerged from this intense experience feeling yet again as if a train had run us over. Exhausted and with so much to process, we crawled into bed and immediately fell asleep.

Chapter 39
Yin Yang

Although the journey had been dark, the next day it was palpable how much transformation had occurred. My body felt more spacious, the energy flowed, and I experienced a new presence within myself, one that was more immersed in life. I had apparently chosen to risk actually taking part fully, to live life after all. Along with this, I released another desire: the desire to reclaim my place as a woman.

I had allowed Marcel to take his place as a man alongside me, but had I also taken my role?

Being a woman. "What does that actually look like?" I asked Annet once as we took our well-known walk through the woods. My friend didn't seem to have an immediate answer, either.

"No idea, Tess. Women have had quite a rough go of it, so what's really left?"

"You know, that emancipation movement, huh? Of course, it was a great aspiration. Women equal to men. But something didn't quite go right. We started thinking that if we are completely the same as men, then we are equal. We have become men!" I said firmly.

"You're right! We've assumed the same roles. Also, being directors of companies, but often not from female values and talents. No, we thought we had to be like those men as much as possible. Otherwise, we wouldn't be seen or appreciated."

"And with all those women who have become men, men can no longer take up their role either…" I mused.

"That explains why we are all still searching for our natural roles. We've all stepped out of them."

"Being a woman, then. How are we going to do that, An? I mean, I can feel what it means: just being, being purely present, letting something emerge from nothing, chaos, softening, slowing down. Not really values that are highly valued right now in the male-dominated world. Just purely being present." I said sadly.

"I don't know if the insurance company where I work now would appreciate me just being present," Annet laughed.

"Remember after my bankruptcy, when I traded in my office life for a studio, some paint, and a few canvases? At that time, I sometimes thought: I'm going to sit in the office with my easel and then brainstorm with people completely freely, moving along with the team. Without a goal, just to be, and it would then become visible how, in this way, together, we could bring magnificent creations into being."

"And? Did you do that then?" Annet looked at me incredulously.

"No, of course I didn't! I didn't dare to do that at all. Just the idea of proposing that to my carefully constructed business network. What would they think?" I laughed. "How brilliant would that have been? I'm one hundred percent sure I would have made a valuable contribution," I told her.

"Yes, but who's going to pay you for that?" Annet asked.

"That remains the eternal nonsense, doesn't it?" I said, somewhat exasperated. "We know something is right, but the money… How am I going to live and stay alive? Because we all wonder that, don't we, An? There has to be bread on the table, money in the coffers, the chimney has to smoke. How do I stay in this fantastic, chaotic, creative flow AND make sure I stay upright in this world?" I sighed deeply. "No idea. But surely it can't be that because of stupid money we're all just going to stop living our essence?"

It remained silent in the forest. Annet had no answer either. I knew this was a tricky one. But certainly not impossible.

"Marcel has indicated that he would like to give me all the space I need to figure this out. He feels it's important that I write that book now and feel free to create. He'll pay the rent when I can't cough it up for a while, so that I can free myself from that money trap." I told her.

"Oh, how nice. Every woman dreams of that, right?" Annet looked at me, slightly jealous.

"Well, it sounds like a lovely idea, but my entire system goes haywire because of it. Getting that space also means trusting in love. For me, money was also about control, my way of making it safe for myself, ensuring that I would always be okay. Will I dare to trust my man, and allow myself to create what wants to be created? Am I going to let myself be truly free? Am I going to let go of my so-called certainties?"

"Yes, that's also part of it, then, isn't it? Daring to surrender to the man as a woman," Annet said, looking doubtful. "Be careful what you wish for," she laughed afterward.

"You know, An, I also feel this is my chance. Now I can try it out. I have a partner who supports me, who really understands what I'm doing, shares the same desire. I'm not going to let this go."

"I'm enthusiastically encouraging you. Go for it!" Annet gave me another big hug and walked back to her cottage after these last words.

For me, the choice was clear. Yes, I was going to take this on. It was important. And for the first time, I also felt the space and safety within myself to dare to do this with a man.

That last session had brought a lot to light, and with it had come a softening. The insecurity was something from the past. Now, I was choosing a new experience. One of being relaxed and carried along by life. So okay, bring it on! And I stepped in.

Chapter 40
Über-Powerful

We were now a few months into the 'experiment'. Of course, it didn't go smoothly right away. I allowed things to happen, then stopped again. I got moving and then hit the brakes hard. Yet, gradually, more peace entered my system, and I could surrender more and more to this new reality. I could now experience that it was safe. Marcel didn't mind that my contribution, like my creativity, was rather chaotic. Financially, things also flowed. There was more than enough income, so that stress disappeared. A new reality unfolded before my eyes.

An ideal situation arose to put what we'd learned into practice. Out of the blue–and those are the best moments–someone coached by Marcel made a proposal. He asked if he could come to us for 24 hours to advance his personal development. He wanted a deeper contact with himself. We both felt a very clear YES to this question.

And for the first time, I could feel how important it was that we were indeed equals, but certainly not the same. This man would benefit most if I engaged in these 24 hours from my feminine essence, and Marcel from his masculine value.

I agreed with Marcel that I would let go of everything, and that I wouldn't think up anything, arrange anything, or need to know anything in advance. I would be pure. Marcel thought that was a good plan, too. No interference with the overview. He would maintain the peace and stability. Create a safe space. That was what he loved best.

On a rainy afternoon, Harold arrived at our home. A well-dressed, handsome man stepped out of his leased Tesla. He was clearly successful, and it radiated from him in every way. Yet, he was with us now because this success did not bring him the satisfaction he had hoped for. Once he'd entered, we introduced ourselves and sat around the kitchen table.

I had prepared a pan of soup so we could connect over a leisurely lunch. From then on, things moved along effortlessly. I felt no pressure and could just be. As a result, I also had a keen sense of what was needed in the moment.

After lunch, Harold's question also became clear. How could he slow down and reconnect with himself?
    Silence, I felt. Silence and letting the subconscious speak.

I suggested a creative exercise; a session in which we both worked on a drawing, but purely intuitively. Every five minutes, we swapped our drawings and continued working. This task involved letting go, allowing whatever emerged on paper, and by not talking, we naturally sank deeper into our bodies, where inner truths often hide.

The afternoon flew by. Moreover, the creative exercise brought many unconscious things to light and, above all, gave Harold an experience he had never had before: creation without thinking. As a result, he felt an increased confidence and a deeper connection with himself, the opposite of what he was used to, with his head constantly in control.

After dinner, we continued the session with an online personality test, which also provided inspiration. This test offered more rational insights into his protective mechanisms and the resulting behaviours; information his mind could use. After these two quite different experiences, he retreated to his own space to let everything sink in.

The next morning, Marcel accompanied him into the woods

for some coaching and exercises that further connected Harold with his body and emotional world. After this walk, I guided him through a meditation where he met his inner child. The safety and trust that had developed over the last few hours enabled him to open up completely and confront his feelings of sadness and loneliness. It was an important step in connecting with himself.

Before we knew it, the 24 hours were over and he drove back out of the park.

To my great surprise, it had all gone really effortlessly. Both perspectives, from both the masculine and feminine, had given Harold a complete picture. He now knew with clarity what his next steps were in his transformation process.

For a moment, I felt guilty about Marcel. It had gone so effortlessly for me, but had I let him do all the work? This question made me think. I was still stuck in the belief that work had to be hard, consume all my energy and, above all, require effort. So, this relaxed way of working did not feel like work to me. The brilliant thing was that Marcel had felt the same relaxation. Because I had not interfered with organisational matters, he had felt all the freedom to take charge.

Wow!
   This was the experience I had longed for but wasn't sure actually existed. So this could come about when men and women truly worked together as equals, seeing each other's distinct qualities, desires, and essences.

Perhaps we could unlock our greatest potential as humanity by embracing our differences! That day, I experienced the masculine and feminine together as über-powerful. What would the world look like if we could bring these two forces more into balance?

Chapter 41
Idyllic Water Mill For Rent

Joining those forces, bringing more and more people into contact with the power within themselves, became increasingly important to us. Marcel and I moved toward a common mission, empowering it with our own talents. He stopped most of his training work with companies to focus completely on personal pathways, retreats, and ceremonies. I dedicated myself entirely to art, which increasingly became a part of the ceremonies as well. I complemented painting with tattoo designs. These designs acted as a kind of talisman, empowering people's transformation processes. Occasionally, we integrated creative therapy into the developmental processes. I also wanted to finish my book.

Increasingly, we also felt that the park where we now lived no longer provided the space we needed to realise our visions. We dreamed of a place where we could have more freedom to organise our ceremonies, host larger groups, and have more space for a yurt for group work in the summer and a studio to fully embrace my art. Space we desperately needed to fully live out what we were meant to do.

About six months earlier, I had a kind of vision about a different place. We were sitting together on the couch discussing one of Marcel's trainings, when an image suddenly flashed before me.
　"We're going to live in a mill," I blurted out.
　Marcel laughed. "Should I pack my boxes now?"
　He joked, but then said, his voice serious now, "Tess, you

can manifest whatever you want, but I want to live here this summer and enjoy the park and the community."

Clear intentions and energy were set, and it was right after the summer that the new place came our way.

We were in Norway for a week of hiking at the end of that summer. On a rest day, after having spent two days climbing mountains, I was casually scrolling through Facebook when a water mill appeared. It was a beautiful spot. Not only was the water mill for rent, but on the property, the owner had also converted a barn into a training room, added extra lodging, and a vegetable garden that would supply fresh ingredients for everyone. She was looking for a couple to rent the water mill.

"This is it," I said to Marcel, holding my phone screen up to his face. "This is the place! Look at it, everything we need to do our work is here. A space where you can hold ceremonies. A conservatory at the water mill, where I can create my art. And all in a place in nature, living with like-minded people."

Marcel grabbed the phone from my hands to take a closer look at the pictures.

"Well, this does indeed feel very good. Are you going to send a message?"

He had not even finished speaking when I snatched the phone back from his hands and quickly typed a message to the owner, whom I didn't know.

Soon she responded, and we introduced ourselves via voice message. It immediately felt very good for everyone. Had we not been in Norway, we would have driven straight there. Instead, we arranged a meeting via Zoom, and when that ended with great enthusiasm, we knew a lot was going to change soon.

And that was true, just not in the way we had imagined…

Everything happened very quickly. Upon returning from Norway, we drove to the place on the same day. Bianca, the owner, greeted us with great enthusiasm and showed us everything. It was beautiful there.

The estate also had a special symbolism: during the liberation in World War II, it served as the headquarters for the Americans, and it was therefore called 'the place of liberation.'

Exactly what we were doing: freeing people. I saw one good sign after another and bounced around the yard with happiness. It appeared everything was set up just for us. Before we knew it, we were brainstorming about joint liberation weekends we could host at this magical place.

Less than three weeks later, we were surrounded by moving boxes, getting ready for our upcoming departure. The weird thing was, as happy as I was with the place, I had a vague, nagging feeling.

"Honey," I said that afternoon as I stood folding another moving box, "it feels like we're not going to live there at all."

My sweetheart looked at me incredulously.

"Yeah, I get that it sounds weird, but that's how it feels."

"Well, we're packing these boxes anyway, and in a week we'll be driving into the yard there," Marcel said, already focusing on something else. That packing, of course, was done with his well-known military precision, and nothing was going to distract him from that.

So, I quickly pushed the restless feeling aside and moved on to the next box as well.

Since we hadn't planned on moving so soon, the planning was chaotic. During the previous week, Marcel had been a guide at a five-day retreat while I was alone at home among packed boxes. This solitude gave the restless feeling even more room to grow. The tension spread through all my muscles, and it wasn't just about the move. What was I feeling anyway?

Halfway through the week of the retreat, Marcel sent a voice message in the app group we had started with Bianca. He talked about his experiences enthusiastically.

He was guiding a group of therapists from all over the world who had come to the Netherlands to learn how they too could use truffles to guide their clients through the process of liberation from trauma, fears, or illness.

So many extraordinary things had occurred. For example, a therapist who had suffered from back pain for twenty years healed himself during a ceremony and walked around pain-free for the first time in all those years. Another man confronted the deeply hidden grief of three miscarriages, which facilitated another process with the men. Much had been healed and shared, and real transformation had taken place.

I heard the emotion in his voice as he talked about it. My man was deeply moved, and that touched me again. When he was doing this work, he connected so well, then love flowed. I enjoyed what he shared.

But for Bianca, this news triggered a tsunami of less positive feelings. She was scared to death. In the days that followed, one panicked message after another arrived in our app group. Was this what we were planning to do? What kind of sessions were these? You really couldn't heal yourself that easily. Were we even grounded in reality? Who would come? What would the neighbours think if we did this here at the water mill?

Fear permeated her messages, and I was shocked because we had just made a commitment to this mission, right? Suddenly, Bianca backtracked, sending messages about the rental period, bringing up a deposit that wasn't previously needed, and apparently eager to end our agreement.

I felt something was not right. When Marcel came home two days later, I immediately burst into tears.

"Honey, I don't know how we're going to do it, but I don't want to go there anymore. It feels so unsafe." I looked at him in a panic.

However, Marcel, who had learned to function under all circumstances and make the impossible possible, simply switched into 'stability mode.'

"Sweetheart, calm down. We're doing this together. We'll be fine. I've already spoken to Bianca briefly. She's a little freaked out, but I'm sure we'll figure it out once we get there. Tess, we're moving tomorrow and nothing's going to change that now," he said firmly.

His calmness made me relax a bit. Maybe I was just a bit emotional about the move and didn't need to take it all so hard. We were going tomorrow. Everything would work out.

The water mill was indeed fantastic, and the conservatory, in which I could create my art, was a dream studio. Paintings flew from my brush. Marcel was also in a tremendous flow. A group of men had emerged from the group of therapists, wanting to start an international company together to conduct more of these types of ceremonies. Marcel would supervise the sessions in the Netherlands. Work flowed in naturally.

We put our energy into every last detail while decorating the water mill beautifully. This place was a wonderful home where we could both relax.

However, outside in the yard, things were different. Bianca felt so much resistance to Marcel's work that he had to look for an offsite location for his ceremonies, as he was no longer welcome in her training room. Almost every week, there was something she didn't like.

Sometimes we hadn't done enough in the yard, or we had posted something on Facebook that she disapproved of. The flow was gone. It was like walking through molasses. No matter how many conversations we had or what we tried, we could not find common ground, until it felt as if we were walking on eggshells every day. Everything suddenly had to be fixed, and her expectations changed by the day.

Less than five weeks later, after yet another conversation with Bianca, it became apparent to me that the situation was untenable.

"Honey," I said to Marcel, "we can't live somewhere where our work faces so much resistance. Her judgments are so harsh and it shouldn't be like this. You aren't able to fully stand your ground here, or even do your work. She scrutinises everything we do. I can hardly breathe. We moved here to give us space, to stop keeping ourselves small. No more compromises, darling. We are in such a flow with the work we're meant to do. But it's definitely not here!"

There, that was out. Relieved, I took a deep breath.

"I know," Marcel said, looking at me calmly. "I have tried to work around it a bit, but it's getting worse. It's time to make choices. I mean, *Walk Your Talk*. I guide everyone to be courageous, to live their full potential. So, I can't sit here holding myself back for fear of losing our home."

He sighed for a moment, realising as I did that a decision had been made already.

"That means packing boxes again in five weeks," he muttered to himself.

I gave him a hug. "Honey, for the right spot, we'll pack those boxes again."

"Yes, we will." He hugged me tightly, too.

"You know, dear," I said after a few minutes, "I feel we can focus our energy on what is really important to us."

We sat down quietly opposite each other, both taking a few deep breaths as we looked into each other's eyes.

"Marcel, the place is already there; we just need to invite it sincerely to present itself?" I looked at him, and both of us felt the energy of embracing the unknown.

"Yes, the new place, THE place for us, may it present itself," Marcel said as he grasped my hands.

I felt the energy flowing, our connection to everything.

Yes, that place was coming.

Chapter 42
Don't Fight: Be Free

It was exciting. We had asked Bianca to come over so we could tell her we no longer felt the match. We didn't know how she would react. For all we knew, things could escalate and we might have to leave this coming weekend.

This was one of those situations where it was tempting to avoid being honest, afraid of the consequences, and perhaps look for something else first. However, that strategy also had consequences. Namely, we would then find ourselves entangled in a web of lies, secrecy, and repressed issues. In that energy, we would fail to create the place that was meant for us.

So, we chose to be honest about it.
    And that also meant being honest about our own part in the whole thing. Because we had indeed overlooked some red flags. We had longed for this place so much that we had walked right past them. Also, we had lost sight of what was really important to the owner and whether that suited us. We laid it all out on the table and invited her to share her story with the same openness. Could we part ways here amicably?

What we hoped for happened. She was relieved. She had also felt a lot of resistance within herself. Actually, it had also become much clearer to her what she now wanted with the place, and it didn't match our vision. And yes, we felt the same. Despite the collective disappointment, relief prevailed. We could all breathe again and relax. We gave her all the space she needed to take the place back, and she gave us the space to find something else.

In the months that followed, things started flowing for all of us. She found the right people for her training room, gained the financial freedom she had longed for all those years, and could work with people who empowered her. Meanwhile, we gained more and more insight into what was important to us. Without the pressure of having to leave, we could freely explore places, talk to people, and truly align our feelings with what was intended.

We learnt that when you stay away from the struggle, you free everyone involved.

Staying away from the battle: Marcel and I sometimes had discussions about that, especially when he got excited about politics or other current affairs issues, such as a 'new' government cabinet, billions being siphoned off, a small group of people getting richer and richer. Whenever something came up that really didn't pass muster, there was intense outrage at first, followed by the temptation to respond angrily online. In other words, a fight.

Injustice also evoked powerful feelings of struggle within me. The news triggered me like a pinball. It was unbearable to witness! Grown men and women lying, cheating, and being self-interested and destructive on so many levels. For me, the biggest challenge was not to react out of anger. I tried with all my might to stay out of the suffocating quicksand of negativity. I aimed not to fight, but to put an energy into the world that matched what I felt was right. And that was certainly not easy when people were at each other's throats all over the media.

How could I stay true to myself and yet stay out of the fray? How could I continue to open my heart when I felt I had to protect it with metre-thick walls? This approach required taking responsibility for my process. It demanded the courage to really see what was happening inside me. What was being triggered? Were my words and actions pure? Were they loving? Or did I actually want to destroy something out of anger?

That was difficult; the line was thin. But it was also everything we needed from each other as human beings in these times: to dare to admit, 'I have no idea either.'

To honestly admit that we just didn't know would have been really refreshing in this day and age. Admitting that everything was new and exciting. That we too often let fear, financial interests, or feelings of inadequacy influence us. And that we were just saying or shouting something: Left or Right, For or Against, even though we didn't really know the answers.

What if we had had the courage to admit it? Wouldn't space have suddenly opened up? Space to open the heart. To truly connect with each other. To see each other and know we are all just here, doing something.

If we had dared to get out of our heads and let go of control, we could have walked right out of this rational prison. If only we had dared to allow the uncomfortable feelings of not knowing, powerlessness, fear, and sadness. Known how to embrace our protective mechanisms in order to lovingly release them. Then, in these times of crisis, with our masks in our hands, we could have truly seen each other for the first time.

And there, in that place of vulnerability, openness, and sincerity, we might have accessed a world of unprecedented possibilities. We could have opened ourselves to innovate and see new alternatives.
    Then, perhaps, we could have created a completely different reality.

Don't fight: be free.

Chapter 43
Leaving The Game Board

The first step was to stop fighting with each other and ourselves. But to truly create a new world, to actually change our reality, the next step was also necessary: leaving the game board.

Suppose you start a game of Monopoly on Christmas Day, and five hours later, your ten-year-old nephew owns all the streets and even gives you another loan to pay the rent. The only thing to do then is to leave the game board! You have nothing more to do there. As long as you continue to roll the dice in his game, you are lost. You will feel more and more frustration, and he will always win! It's time to congratulate him on his win and join the people in the kitchen who had long since left the board.

"Well, back to today's reality, Tessa."
   Annet had found our water mill after a ninety-minute drive, and it was our first time walking in nature again. She had listened to my Monopoly analogy and was sceptical.

"We have a world stage dominated by governments and big corporations where we feel the same powerlessness. Being pushed around. Like we can do anything about that?" she said with an incredulous look.

"Yes, we can," I replied firmly. "Even in this reality, we can leave that game board. We don't have to join their game! I think that's the opportunity we have. I mean, how much crazier does it have to get before we throw the dice on the board and decide to do something else?"

"Well, a lot crazier, I guess," Annet said, "because I haven't seen a real uprising yet. Yes, there are strikes, and a group chains themselves to a private jet or throws a gallon of tomato soup over a work of art. But it's not a mass uprising. We don't really upend the board, even though we're pretty shortchanged as humans."

"Annet, look, a group of people have decided this is the game. They've laid out a board, positioned some pawns, and devised game rules. Rules that they are very happy with. If you then join their game and you don't like the game, you can sit around the board stamping your feet, throwing tomato soup, but you will never win. After all, you are playing their game with their rules, and left or right, you remain the loser. It is their game! If you fight with them about that game, you remain in their story, and you maintain a dynamic of victim and perpetrator for all eternity."

"And so?" Annet looked at me questioningly.

"I was thinking, what if all those millions of people who are so angry right now took their attention away from that game altogether? And what if they focused that attention on themselves, went inward, really started feeling who they are, started feeling how they would like to live? What if everybody focused all that attention and energy on that? Purely on that, without being busy with the outside world, without thinking about how, just feeling and setting the intention. What a mega-impact that would have! Reality would change on the spot."

"Yes, I think so too. What you give attention to grows. But how on earth are we going to do that?" Annet asked me.

"I think right now we are invited to really connect with each other. Not from a shared victimhood or in a battle of us against them, but connect with our deep values, with that which really drives us, with who we really are. That would put an enormously powerful field in the world. And stories that don't resonate with that will then be completely unnourished and disappear like snow in the sun."

"I understand what you're saying, Tess, but we still have no idea how to shape the world."

"But that doesn't mean it can't be done," I objected. "It 'only' requires a dose of courage, curiosity about the unknown, making real contact with each other, daring to admit a deep desire, and a craving for adventure."

"Yes, an adventure, that's definitely going to be it then!" exclaimed Annet, laughing. "How are we going to get ourselves there? We are conditioned very differently. Through our upbringing, education, the media, family, friends. It feels like a tight suit in which I walk through life with my throat squeezed shut. I sometimes think there's no other way."

I stopped walking and looked at Annet.

"If you really stop for a moment, do you truly feel that this is our maximum potential as human beings? That we cannot do better than what we see in the world now? Don't you feel that so much more is possible? That we long for a world of authenticity, connection with each other, where we create to truly contribute and empower the talents within ourselves. Away from uniformity and the comatose consuming lifestyle."

"Yes, of course," Annet confirmed. "But it just feels so far away."

"It's high time we freed ourselves from our limiting thoughts and beliefs. We should disentangle ourselves and explore. Inside ourselves, that is! If we can feel ourselves again, then we can also start seeing that our potential as humanity is infinitely greater, and we will begin to long for this more and more. Then that inner fire can no longer be dampened, and we will spontaneously ignite the dormant sparks around us. We will collectively be infinitely powerful, and then, then we will truly start living life again."

"That would be true liberation!" exclaimed Annet, now also enthusiastic.
   "No more fighting an old system, old fears, or beliefs. Freeing myself from the shackles within myself and then daring to follow my own path in a world I think has gone mad." Annet suddenly danced a few steps through the forest like a woodland elf.

"Okay, now you're officially off the track," I joked.

Laughing, we walked back to the property together, and the water mill came into view again. Both of us were excited about the glimpse into another future. Would it really be possible?

Chapter 44
Don't Rock The Boat

During our quiet Sunday mornings in the watermill, Marcel regularly read something inspiring or striking. It was during such a relaxing breakfast that he came up with a quote from Václav Havel:

'The real question is whether the brighter future is always so distant. What if it had been here for a long time already, and only our own blindness and weakness have prevented us from seeing it around us and kept us from developing it?'

I looked up briefly from peeling my just-boiled egg when he started talking about Havel's view.

"I think this is exactly where we are right now, love. I think as a human race, we really need to look at things differently now, to see what's actually been there all along, so that we can innovate."

"Yes, I know," I said as I put my spoon in my egg. "But in recent years, we've been pushed so much into fear that we've fallen into survival mode, and that's disastrous for innovation. Fear actually creates tunnel vision, a need for frames, black-and-white thinking, duality. Well, that's exactly what we see happening all day now."

"Tess, we as humanity are capable of so much more! Did you know that there are already people who know how to create free energy? That there are healing methods that don't involve a pill? That there are agricultural methods that do not deplete the soil but make it fertile? If only people knew we can expand our minds so that we really do think outside the box and develop even more cool innovations."

I had to laugh at my man's enthusiasm; this was exactly where we had once found each other. I heartily agreed with him, of course. But before I could agree, he continued.

"Why aren't we hearing about this every day on the talk shows? Why aren't we embracing these innovations en masse? Why aren't we setting up one research centre after another to improve our resources and make them available to everyone? Why aren't we immediately making sure we live in a better world?"

Did I hear a slight frustration in the voice of the man who normally wouldn't let anything get him down? I looked at him and responded dryly, "Because all these things have something in common, dear. They don't make money for anybody. Nobody will line their pockets."

"Exactly!" Marcel replied. "If we embraced these developments, it would liberate the entire world population at once. People would no longer have to survive and work as a cog in a soul-destroying system. Instead, they could choose for themselves. And then, that thoroughly rotten money system would lose its modern slaves."

"Yes, that's it," I agreed.

"You know what I heard this week?" Without waiting for my response, he continued eagerly. "The CEO of a major electronics company mentioned in an interview last week how he saw a feasible plan for an epidemic hospital fail, because hospital executives didn't want to share their 'trade.' Yes, you heard correctly. Sick people are trade! The success of market forces in healthcare!"

I had to laugh at his passion and added to it.

"I know, darling, and there are many more examples like that. Surely how we treat each other must have become unsightly to everyone by now!"

I left my egg untouched to list on my fingers what had been irritating me immensely for so long:

"MPs running away from a vote to appreciate care workers a little better. Why aren't these people paid properly in the first place?

Then we have youth care with such long waiting lists that you are an adult before you receive help, that's if you make it at all.

Moreover, constitutional laws are often disregarded, and no judge may voice any objection.

And this one: relying on the judgment of 'objective' consultants in a crisis, who propose a solution while shamelessly making a lot of money off that solution. They then appear on talk shows, getting all the space to present, with a straight face, their solution as the only solution. I mean, where is the critical journalism?

Of course, we also have companies that don't pay taxes. Do I need to say more?"

I had a lot to say about this, so I continued.

"All those people who work forty hours a week and can't afford housing.

Not to mention the fact that we are in a healthcare crisis, and there is virtually no focus on healthy living! I sometimes fantasise that two years ago, besides all the Covid measures, the government had started a health programme, with tax breaks on healthy eating and exercise. To inspire the entire population to achieve a healthy BMI. Anyway, I digress...

This list could become endless. We stand by and watch," I concluded sternly.

"You know what surprises me the most?" Marcel asked

without waiting for an answer. "Except for an afternoon of protest and an excited Twitter feed, there is no real uproar. No real uproar. No major strike action. How can it be that so much is happening that really doesn't serve us as humanity anymore, but which is just allowed to happen, and by us?"

"Oh, the answer is simple, my sweet." He looked at me questioningly.
"Don't rock the boat."
"What?"
"Just don't start rocking that boat. We close our eyes tight, wishing what we've long felt in our guts isn't true. We don't want to admit that our society has gradually become a festering, open wound.

Because then things start to fray, really hurt, cause discomfort...
it's still a little too comfortable.
There's still too much to lose.
That fine house you really want to keep, which is worth a lot now.
That salary every month in the bank that eases a lot of the discomfort.
You don't want to create hassle because you don't have the energy for that anymore!
What if nothing is right anymore?
Does everything collapse?
And what will I do then?
So...

DON'T ROCK THE BOAT!"

"It's a bit like having an abusive partner," I enthusiastically continued my account. "You may get a black eye from him, but he's so sweet to the kids, pays the bills, and can actually have good days.

But after a while, it hurts too much somewhere, right? You can't sell it to yourself anymore that it's still okay. Deep down in your cells, you know: it's not right anymore, it's so not right!"

"Yes, exactly!" agreed Marcel enthusiastically. "Let's rock the f*^ing boat!"

"Anyway, fear rules, and humanity seems to be stuck. So there's no rocking of that boat at all," I said, somewhat dully. "And since we apparently don't dare to consciously choose to live more freely, something else is happening."

Marcel looked at me questioningly.
   "The collective, humanity, is choosing unconsciously. For destruction. How brilliant is that!" I exclaimed enthusiastically. After all, I now had a sneaky fascination with the end of the world.

"Even though I am not looking forward to the coming time, I can feel that it is necessary. The crises are coming in rapid succession, the straps will soon cut even further into our skin. We are going to make ourselves so incredibly uncomfortable that we will have to struggle out of that too-tight suit."

Marcel now understood where I was going and let me continue talking quietly.

"If the chaos is big enough, there is only one way not to go completely crazy: go back to the place where the answer is clear. Where you will always know if something is right or wrong. A place so pure that the need for struggle and being right fall away.

A knowing within yourself that goes beyond thinking, a deeper layer of feeling. Where you just are, and you feel your truth vibrating through all your cells.

Feeling more than talking.

Knowing more than thinking."

I took a breath, but I hadn't finished yet. "I dream of a world where we all dare to make this connection again. To feel and embrace our truth. To dare to live again from this autonomous state of being. Powerfully connected to ourselves and thus to each other.

There we will laugh, deep from our bellies, at the absurdity of everything. We will experience how ingeniously we are connected to each other, and therein lies the infinite power to create a world far beyond our wildest fantasies.

Because from this authenticity, this purity, we can create the most incredible visions of a new world with our diverse perspectives and ideas.

Being and feeling.

Being and connecting.

Being and loving.

We are so close…"

"And yes," I concluded my speech with a meaningful look, "it takes chaos, a big fat crisis, a world that seems to be going crazy. There is no other way, and we are creating this together. Because deep, deep down inside, we long for this so much. We are going to make it worse and worse until we really can't do anything else but finally break through.

To the essence, to ourselves."

"Nice ending, dear." Marcel wiped the shell of my just-peeled egg off the table. "Are you putting all this in your book, though?"

Oh yes, that book... Indeed, it was about time I picked up the laptop again.

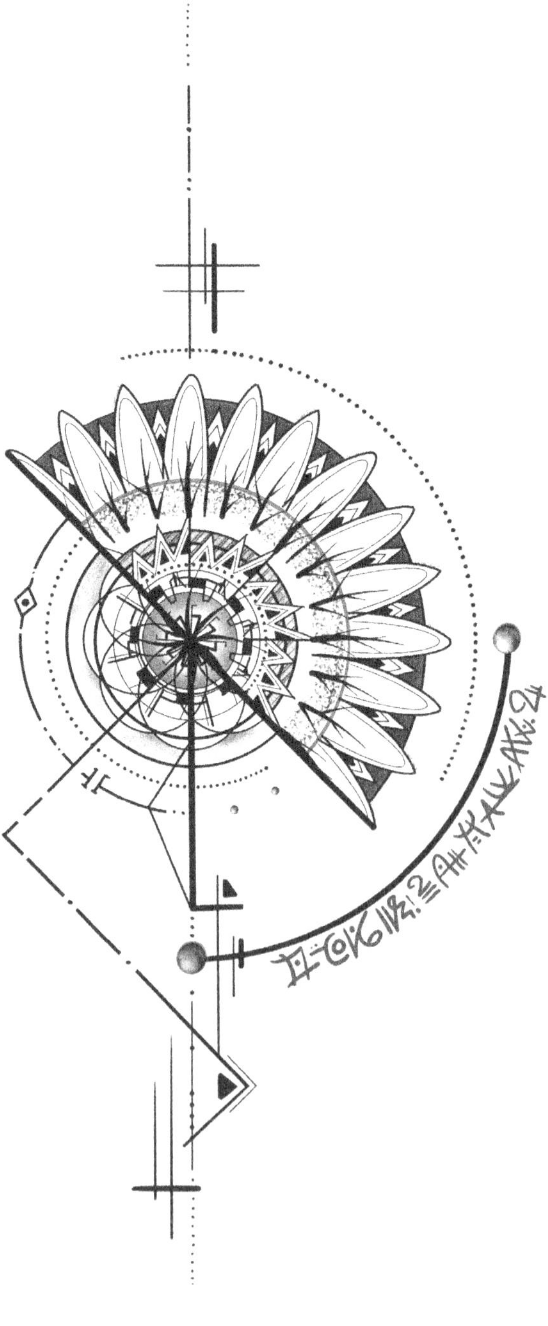

Chapter 45
Courageous People

So the crises that seemed to follow each other every day now provided a wonderful opportunity to do things differently. And didn't we all long for an alternative? Something new? That which did not yet exist, but was already sort of palpable. Who was going to be the first to take that step?

"Courageous people." That's what Marcel always called the people who came to him for a coaching programme, or truffle journey. People who dared to really open themselves up to everything outside the existing concepts and frameworks. People who wanted to experience how big their impact in the world could really be.

Brave they were, because once they got a taste of that new experience, there was no going back. It often led to major changes in their lives, work, or relationships.
So there was a lot to lose, especially much of the old, of the certain. And if they did not yet know what they were getting in return, and it was unknown what was coming next, yes, then they needed a lot of courage to take that step. Especially when the world around them continued spinning in the old way.

"Yes, they are certainly brave people." Annet looked at me seriously. It had been a long time since she had come our way for a walk. I missed our daily wanders in the woods immensely and was glad she was back.

"Tess, it's one thing to feel and experience this. It's another entirely to actually start living by it. Especially in this society, where people claim they want us to be authentic, but at the first glimpse of authenticity, they bring out the pitchforks to push others back into the box."

"Annet, going back in the box is no longer an option at all once you have experienced all that is possible. Then you can only go one way, and that is forward."

"Yes, but how?" sighed Annet as we rounded the corner into the woods.

"By just living step by step yourself in a new way. Even if it's super small movements, as long as we move in that direction." My hands extended forward to reinforce the movement toward the future a little more.

"I do it that way myself. Staying in the here and now every day, present, in touch with all of us, the field. And then giving myself the space to always follow impulses, no matter how illogical. When I do that, I always experience brilliant experiences and encounters," I explained.

"Yes, I always find how you do that super inspiring, but I'm not sure I'm quite ready for that yet."

"And that's why we have to share this too, Annet!" I rattled on enthusiastically as we walked briskly toward the moor.

"It's so important that we share our experiences. That we don't just sit and wait. We have to dare to raise our heads above that level. Our stories are empowering for everyone around us. Then even more people dare. Then even more people will feel that there is an alternative that will make everyone a lot happier. By sharing, experimenting, and connecting. Then this new reality comes into being literally before our eyes. There are dozens of examples of that."

A look of recognition crossed Annet's face, and she made a little hop. "That's so true. I saw a video of an interview with a businesswoman on LinkedIn yesterday. She burst into tears.

She had just remodeled her business two years ago, which meant she couldn't claim financial support. And then there was another lockdown, so she couldn't save it, not even with all the will in the world."

"Oh yes, I saw that too! With the director of a transport company who then wanted to help her immediately with ten thousand euros. I think he wrote: 'Why shouldn't we entrepreneurs who have it good just help the other one?'

And he just did it, huh! Put his money where his mouth was. He made ten thousand euros available and invited his fellow entrepreneurs to do the same. His post went viral!"

"Yes, and the government was nowhere to be seen. So many people think we live in a welfare state, but that is no longer the case," Annet muttered.

"But that's also the beauty of this situation," I responded to her point. "Precisely because the government did not help this lady, a situation arose that we hadn't seen before. Now this businesswoman could feel that she was not alone, that there was indeed a connection between them, and a desire to support each other. She experienced that she didn't need the government at all. Because, let's face it, this so-called welfare state has been a monstrosity for years, with the benefits affair being the icing on the cake."

"Down with the rules, conditions, and controllers!" I shouted firmly, as we turned from the heath back into the woods.

"Away with the welfare state?" Annet looked at me questioningly. "Tess, you can't just do that, can you? No more controlling bodies at all? I think people will abuse it then!"

"Annet, I think it is precisely these beliefs that lead us to create such a terrible controlling system. Distrust until proven otherwise. If you take that as your starting point, everyone who needs a little help feels like a criminal before they've even received a euro. And guess what? If you are in that corner, you often start behaving accordingly, to some extent. And so, before we know it, we have created with our fear that which we were so afraid of: everyone is cheating. It's a pretty vicious cycle."

"Yes, you have a point there, but I don't see how we can really do this differently yet." Annet picked up a stick and knocked a few leaves off the trees here and there.

"It requires really connecting," I said firmly. "If we truly connect and then feel what the right action is, we can start following our intuition. Then we don't need to set down any rules either, because that businesswoman really isn't going to take advantage of anything. That director doesn't need any conditions for his loan at all. In this way.

Such trust results in a situation that is best for all of us. Maybe she can pay back quickly, and she will be happy to do so because everything is so open and without frameworks. And she, in turn, after this positive experience, is going to help someone else. Or maybe repaying is difficult, but if we look at the bigger picture, she can continue to make her contribution to our society thanks to the help she received. Perhaps that director will see her contribution reflected in a completely different way: in a nice client portfolio, for example, because this is such an inspiring story."

"Isn't that a pipe dream?" Annet asked. I could see I hadn't quite got my friend on board with this idea yet.

"Do you follow the posts of Michelle van Tongerloo, that young GP and street doctor at St. Paul's Church in Rotterdam?" I asked her.

"Yes, I think I've seen that one pass by once."

"Well, she does exactly this. She writes about everything that makes little sense to her, and shares it on LinkedIn. It's truly toe-curling to read what she writes. She is constantly dragged into a quagmire of bureaucracy in her work. Institutions point fingers at each other, costs skyrocket, and patients still don't get proper help.

But the great thing is that in addition to sharing her outrage, she immediately proposes a clear and simple alternative. For example, she had a homeless man with a leg injury. The hospital sent him away after treatment. The shelter could not help him, and she knew if this man had to let his wound heal on the street, she'd be amputating his leg in a month. Absolutely no one benefits from that. Everyone who read that post felt and knew that this is only worse for us as a society, for human beings. So, she suggested arranging a month's hotel stay for this man. No conditions, no rules, just help. And guess what? That amount was in her account within five minutes.

And this is how she does it every day. With every post, she denounces our current healthcare system. She describes yet another completely illogical and distressing situation. Everyone feels the injustice and nonsense in these stories, and immediately wants to help with money, services, or goods. And all without forms, rules, or controlling authorities."

"Yes, how cool!" Annet almost bounced with each step through the forest. "That reminds me of the initiator of supermarket FRIS, Abdelhamid Idrissi. Do you know him?"
"No, tell me!"
"He opened a store where all the products are free for people living in poverty."
"A kind of food bank?" I asked.
"No, this is a new way. He doesn't just help them put food on the table in the short term. He also wants them to be able to create a better life for themselves in the long run. So, besides daily groceries, they all get coaching. And three guesses what he did?"

Annet looked at me defiantly.

"Well?"

"All without rules, forms, or conditions."

"Oh wow, then he didn't fund this with a government grant."

"No, of course not. Then this wouldn't be possible at all. He raised the money with his story and pure intention through a crowdfunding campaign."

"Yes, you see! This is already happening; there are dozens of examples. All sparks that if we just start seeing and experiencing enough of them, have the potential to start a bonfire. This is how the new world arises naturally, without inventing, imposing rules, or framing ourselves. Beyond fear."

By now, we were walking back into the watermill parking lot. "Courageous people, then," Annet nodded and walked toward her car.

"Courageous people," I confirmed. "People who dare to look at our way of life with a completely open mind. The visionaries who take the first step toward a new world with no idea what it will soon look like."

"Amen," Annet laughed, as she opened the car door and prepared to get in.

"Maybe I'd like to come on one of those inner journeys soon, stretch that mind a little."

"Yes! Shall we go together?"

"Will do!"

And as I watched her drive away and walked back to the water mill, I thought of all those brave people. If we could connect them somehow, how powerful would their impact be?

Chapter 46
Dissenters And Visionaries

The idea of bringing together like-minded people, new thinkers, and doers never left me.

"Honey, what if we could create that place? A safe haven for dissenters, for visionaries?"

Marcel looked at me, smiling. "Absolutely! I've been dreaming of that for years too. We have to start bringing them together. But our place just isn't there yet, dear."

"I know, but I was thinking, surely we can invite these people here, just at our kitchen table. I'm enormously curious to see what will emerge."

"What a good idea! We could start with the people who have all done a truffle trip. Then, they could also share that experience with each other."

"Exactly! For some, I think it's quite difficult to do that at home, with friends and family who have no idea what it's all about."

"Don't say that. You can't go around every dining room table talking about your true potential, the light of humanity, or your delivery of the universe in song." At those last words, he winked at me.

"Giving birth to the universe? Are you crazy or something?" We both burst out laughing.

I realised perfectly well that we were lucky to be both working on this and could share everything with each other. But not everyone had that. So, the idea of a dinner at our home sounded like music to my ears. Together, we scrolled through our calendars that afternoon to set a first date. That same evening, Marcel emailed an invitation to all former participants.

Two weeks later, I was cooking for fifteen people on a Saturday. After an entire morning of cutting, stirring, and kneading, the main dishes were ready. I quickly changed my clothes and checked all the pots and pans.

"Honey, can I help you with something?" Marcel walked behind me into the kitchen and gave me a hug.

"No, dear, you just handle the reception and organisation. I like to focus on the food," I said as I chopped the parsley for the soup and then wiped my hands. "It's just about ready."

"I already see the first guest coming; I'm going to open up!" Marcel said and energetically trotted back out of the kitchen.

I stirred the soup some more and checked my famous meatballs in satay sauce. This is going to be another fun evening, I thought to myself as I set the glasses down on the table and opened the first bottle of wine.

After an hour, when we were all seated at the table and everyone had filled their plates, the stories flowed as naturally as the wine.

"I just said I don't do performance reviews anymore," Margret, a woman in her 50s who worked as a director at a large electronics company, told me.

"So, how did they respond to that?" asked Harm in surprise. He ran his own business and eagerly absorbed all the new ideas.

"I told them how I want to manage my team through connecting from my heart. That I saw a fresh approach from a human perspective: if someone is not performing well, they really don't have to wait for a formal conversation. I immediately sit down with them openly and connectedly. And in my experience, if you do that sincerely, you can always work it out."

The table had become quiet by now, listening intently to this courageous lady.

"I don't know if I can manage 'working from my heart,' with all the alpha males in my office," Harm said jokingly.

"Well, it takes courage to have a face-to-face conversation with your supervisor, but actually, my experience is that if you really do that, everyone is keen to take off their mask. And then the best conversations happen. But yes, you have to dare to take the first step yourself."

Challengingly, she looked at him.

"You're absolutely right," he reluctantly admitted. "I also felt it all during my journey with the truffle. I could experience how connected we were to each other, and how all the nonsense melted away like snow in the sun, which was wonderful!" agreed Harm.

Margret nodded in agreement. "Look, it requires you to be genuinely curious about the other person. To make yourself vulnerable in the process. Not just to be concerned with your own interests, but to be genuinely interested in the person in front of you and what is best for the company. Then it's not so hard at all to get to the right point with someone. But if I hide behind HR protocols, where every form of emotion has been stripped away, the other person thinks: nobody really cares, so I just do what I want."

"Exactly, then they throw their hands up in despair. Those HR problems cost tons of money, by the way," Harm responded dryly.

A woman across the table joined Margret in her story.

"Beautiful! Daring to say no to what you feel is no longer right, regardless of the consequences. So, I quit my job."

With a smiling face, she let out a sigh of relief.

"It felt so out of sync with who I really am."

"How cool!" Jasper, a dentist who had just taken over a practice, gave her a round of applause.

"At my practice, we started doing things differently too…"

Before I could hear more of the story, I saw it was time to clean up and prepare dessert. In the background, I could hear how one person's story stirred up another person's experience, and so the evening naturally filled with inspiring stories of how they had begun to approach life differently.

A father, who was normally very strict with his children, had openly shared what the trip had done to him. After which, the children honestly shared that they also experimented from time to time. Suddenly, there was openness and since then, the family feels much more connected to each other.

Another had cut the cord and sold his business. A business solely focused on making a lot of money no longer gave him the satisfaction it had before. He now wanted to put something meaningful into the world with his money and was currently immersing himself in regenerative agriculture.

A third now viewed his relationship so differently that the connection had become much more loving. His wife had already enthusiastically texted Marcel to express how happy she was with the changes in her husband.

It was empowering to share these experiences. All this openness resulted in beautiful connections, and everyone felt supported in continuing on their new path, with even talk of new collaborations. So, it was late when the last guest got into his car and drove home.

"I can't wait until we have a place of our own where people can stay too," I mused about the evening as I stood drying off a pan and Marcel reloaded the dishwasher.

"Me neither, dear. I feel we can make a move toward that really soon," he replied as he closed the dishwasher door and pressed start.

"We could do so many more wonderful things with these people. Inspiration sessions, brainstorming with each other about innovations, new ways of working, new entrepreneurship," I enthusiastically told him, listing a whole array of ideas.

Marcel laughed out loud and gave me a big kiss on the forehead.

"You're never short of ideas, my love. Now let's make contact first with the place where all this may take place."

Chapter 47
Just Letting The Future Emerge

Beautiful, of course, all those ideas about being open-minded in life, really connecting, letting everything emerge in surrender. Now that I was writing a book about that, I had to live it myself. And reality could be quite unruly.

Even though we had an agreement with Bianca, and the space to create a new place, after several months, we felt it was time to go and agreed on a date of departure. A conversation with Bianca revealed she had indeed been walking around for several weeks with the feeling that we needed to leave. So, our feelings were right. We agreed to leave the house in a month.

We had no idea where we were going. We had seen some pleasant options: farms with land, small parks, or camping grounds. These, of course, required serious financing. But we also felt: we're not going to do this the old way. Not with an anonymous bank or investor who was only concerned with grabbing even more money for himself or his shareholders. At least, we would no longer facilitate that financial pressure and inequality.

This heart-centred choice obviously had consequences. We couldn't just buy a house; it required a whole different kind of partnership. We had announced a while before that we were looking for 'shareholders' people who resonated with our mission, who felt it was important to develop that place and didn't want the highest return in cash for their financing. These were people who really wanted to help build something new, where what they would get in return could take many forms.

People around us became increasingly curious, expressing interest and asking if we could tell them a little more about the place.

We needed something to make our dream palpable and tangible to others. So, I dusted off my laptop again and started building a one-page website. On it, we outlined our dream, mission, desires, ideas about the place, and the team we wanted to work and live with.

After several evenings of feeling and writing together, our plan was finally in place. Not only did we now have something to send to interested parties, but I also felt that we had brought our mission into the energy of the field, expressing a clear YES to this desire, our collaboration, and the future place.

And sometimes, that's all it takes…

"You're already packing boxes, but you don't know where you're going yet?" Annet had come our way for the last time and stood looking around my studio in amazement.

"Yes, it's like old times again; I'm surrendering, trying to let go of control and let what's intended emerge," I sighed.

"Pff, rather you than me. I like to know where I stand three weeks in advance, anyway."

"I basically do, too, you know. But I'll tell you something worse."

Annet looked at me curiously.

"I was walking through the woods this week, trying to relax completely. To turn off my busy thinking head for a moment and feel what was really meant. And then I felt something:

the intention is that you literally won't have a home when you leave on June 1." I raised my left eyebrow meaningfully.

"Oh, gosh!" exclaimed Annet. "How do you deal with so much uncertainty?"

"Well, not always very well either, you know. Then I get a pain in my stomach and feel my body tense up. Sometimes I just cry out the fear. It bothers me more than Marcel. He is very calm. And that helps, too. I really know that we are completely okay together, whatever happens."

"But how does that work in practice? Don't you do anything at all?"

"Well, no, we have seen dozens of places and houses in the last few weeks. But there's a fundamental condition: we really have to feel a collective YES and not just do it out of fear. Not an easy task when impending homelessness looks you in the eye."

"Don't say that," Annet said, looking at me with concern. "Was there really nothing in between so far, then?"

"It seems almost right every time. For example, we came across a beautiful detached house in Enschede, but we knew we couldn't carry out our full dream there. Then we came across another beautiful place. We almost rented it, except that the real estate agent wanted so many documents from us that for a moment we thought we would have to hand over our firstborn as well in order to rent it. So, we politely declined. In Limburg, we walked through a chapel with a monastery, but the owner was nowhere to be seen. And at the last place, we walked ankle-deep in mud and knew that the next ten years would consist of rebuilding. They were all beautiful places, with a lot of potential, but just short of a YES."

"A bit like me scrolling through Tinder," Annet joked.

I laughed out loud along with her. "Yes, and you shouldn't be seduced by the potential you see there, either. No, when what you see is really 'it', then you feel a YES."

"You're right, otherwise before you know it, you'll spend

another six months pouring your energy into a bottomless pit."

"Exactly, then I'd rather sit in a caravan this summer. Anyway, Marcel won't let me say that out loud; he's convinced that special things are going to happen in the coming weeks."

"I hope so, for your sake! Anyway, first things first, what can I pack?"

As I hand Annet a box and some tape a moment later, I mutter, "Let the magic begin."

Besides the superficial excitement, it was also unusually quiet inside me. I trusted that exactly what was intended was going to happen and had surrendered to that thought.

On the day of our move, Marcel unexpectedly received a message. Through word of mouth, someone had heard about our plans and felt he needed to connect with us. He knew a place, a special location in Drenthe, with a financier, a farm with a few homes, and ten hotel rooms. Were we interested in stopping by?

Chapter 48
The Creation Of A New Reality

And now you have arrived at the final chapter. This is the end of my story, the story so far, that is. I hope that with this book, I have been able to take you into a world of unprecedented possibilities–a reality that exists when you dare to surrender to that which you do not know. Here, you can feel a freedom that is not about everything happening around you, but instead about the space you dare to give yourself to be completely who you are.

Because therein lies the creation of our new reality, if we all dare to feel and allow that it already exists.

In which we claim our place,
going through the fire for who we are,
as fully human beings with an open heart,
where you feel: this is real, here I do not doubt for a second,
freed from all the chains in your head.

Does it make you curious already?

Curious about what happens when it all starts flowing within you? When you take off the cap and allow oxygen in? Afraid of an explosion? Of that big fire? Well, brace yourself; you can count on it happening
    Don't be afraid of the explosion. Because after the explosion, there is air, there is space, there is light. The mess is gone, the nonsense of what you think you have to do, gone. A blank canvas presents itself, giving you the chance to live what you've desired for so long.

Dear human being, I want to see you; I want to feel you. I want to experience what it is that you have come to live. What are you experiencing?

For me, this book is a call to myself and to the world. An invitation to that great longing that lies smouldering within all of us. Can we feel what wants to arise? Dare we to ignite it?

A call, because we are already there, we already feel it, we already do it, but so restrained, so constrained, so inhibited and misunderstood.

Feel, feel, feel what is alive.
Dare to live.

And yes, I know, it's all very exciting.
Lying in your bed, bathed in sweat,
panic attacks overwhelming you.
Afraid of death, with infinity in sight,
afraid of the light where the same feeling lurks.

There, where you plunge headfirst into your fear, I have recently discovered something beautiful. That place, where you think, 'Now I can't take it anymore, now it becomes too much for me, this is not for me.' Right in that moment, all alone in bed, in the darkness of the night.
    There. That is the moment where, if you dare, you can let go and say, "Bring it on! Yes, yes, yes, yes! Bring it fucking on, bring it on with what will come, bring me all the fear, give me more panic. Bring it on!!!"

And then, you will find it is gone. Driven away by courage, by complete surrender, by wanting nothing more, by feeling full. There it is gone, and you gain space, beyond your fear and beyond the panic.

We need you. You really have no idea right now what effect

your action will have. But the ripple effect of everyone living their true potential is guaranteed to be enormous. You may not always see it yourself yet, but what really matters is that you take that one necessary step.

This sense of interconnectivity is so strong for me; it can move me to tears to see that we all have this within us and that it is so close.

When we dare to take that first vulnerable step,
reminding ourselves of who we are,
in connection with each other.

Let the magic begin!

Afterword

Not everything in this book is one hundred percent truthful. For reading pleasure, I have sometimes combined characters and placed stories in a different timeline. I have also anonymised people and locations. But everything is based on truth!

I'm still with Marcel. I now devote myself full-time to my art and writing, while he welcomes people from all over the world who want to make beautiful inner journeys. Our ceremonies have evolved into longer personal trajectories, and after a spontaneous inquiry about relationship therapy, we now also guide couples together. Connecting with oneself is one thing, but entering into a love relationship is really the next level. We continue to navigate this process daily, and I can already feel a third book brewing on this subject ;-).

And where are we now? Okay, here's a little update: It's mid-August 2023.

My hunch was right. There was no new house on June 1. Our belongings went into storage, and with no fixed abode, we vacationed in Spain for three weeks. Then it was back to my sister's house one more time. Of course, I wondered if we might be meant to find a place in Spain? But there was nothing to suggest that, so we returned.

The new place in Drenthe? We went to see it. It turned out to be special. A beautiful farmhouse, exactly as we had described in our plan. However, it belonged to someone who had no intention of selling or renting the place. The bizarre thing was, different people repeatedly pointed us to this place. We made multiple visits, and together we exchanged deep desires and visions of the future with the owner.

This is what all three of us felt: we did not know what we had to do with each other, but it was abundantly clear that we were meant to come here. And that was it. That was all we all felt deep inside–that our presence was requested, but we had a no more information than that. The three of us decided to embark on this adventure in complete freedom and without expectations.

This special place is located exactly in the area where the 'freebooters colony' used to be–an area where people were exiled, who did not want to conform to the rules of the Netherlands' colonies. Here, they could throw off the yoke of rules and virtue and build a new life in complete freedom.

And in freedom, it is.

I have believed for years that freedom is the gateway to unprecedented possibilities.
    So we stepped in. We said yes to this adventure and have now been living in this more than magical place for a month. We have no idea for how long or why. I don't think I have ever stepped into anything so openly. We sincerely feel that any outcome is okay, whether it is for a week or for years. We really have no expectations or thoughts about it.

A mental blank canvas,
where everything is allowed to emerge.
A creation that may be beyond our wildest expectations.
Bring it on!

Wherever Marcel and I are, we're going to bring more like-minded people together, anyway. Because we need each other! These connections will create another ripple effect. Besides the dinners, I also think it would be great to organise gatherings after the launch of this book with readers who feel inspired and want to connect, and are also curious about the magic that may happen. I dream of our tribe, our home, and can already feel the tremendous power that will be released here.

How and what? No idea. And that is also the intention. In surrender, in connection with what serves us all, I will let myself be surprised by what will arise.

I know, I mustn't meddle in the process. The first step that had to be taken by me was this book. For years, during meditations and ceremonies, I wrote down the same thing every time: 'Write that book!'

Here it is. ;-)

And with this, I can let go, because it has been set in motion. I've no idea where it will lead, but it is right.

It is up to you now to also take your place on this beautiful earth and to join us in what we, as humanity, have always been capable of: the creation of heaven on earth.

Acknowledgements

This book would not have come about without the unwavering support–and above all, the motivational pushes–of my dear friends and family. Special thanks to my sweetheart, Marcel Dekker, who took on all the financial burdens in the last months of writing to completely free me up so I could focus entirely on writing. But more importantly, he understood how vital this book was to me and the readers. He chose not to read a word of it until the printed version arrived, because he wanted me to be able to write our stories shamelessly and freely. Thank you for your trust!

My fellow readers, Linda Tops, Antoinet Koster, and Marleen Smits, whose enthusiasm and critical eye gave me another push in the right direction. And, of course, my editor, Marlies Vink, whom I magically met (of course) and who turned out to be the perfect choice for linguistically refining this book. Also, the English editor, Eleanor McKenzie, who seemingly out of nowhere, turned out to be the perfect match for the translation.

The cover was a co-creation with a designer, Ruben Lourens, who really dared to create with me and understood from the first moment what I wanted to convey. It was like working on a painting together. I am incredibly happy that together we could realise the cover that I had envisioned, but had no idea how to execute. Thank you, Ruben, for your patience, openness, and creativity!

At the last minute, I also changed printers because I felt something was wrong. Completely out of the blue, I discovered SchultenPrint. The owner, Eric Schulten, immediately felt a connection with the book, and you can see that in the attention and energy he put into printing it. Fortunately, I followed my intuition here as well.

And last, but definitely not least, all the people who bought this book through the presale crowdfunding campaign. Because of your support, I could publish the book myself and print the first edition.

This book belongs to all of us!

Especially for you

Are you curious about where we are now, the activities we organise, and how to connect with like-minded people? I thought it would be fun to create a page for you, the reader of my book, featuring reactions from other readers, photos that accompany the true story, interesting links, answers to frequently asked questions, and information on upcoming events.

Visit this page at: www.tessasmits.com/readers

Printed in Great Britain
by Amazon